Trading Currencies: Taking a Step Further in Your Trading Career

I0486072

Table of Contents

Introduction

A lot of people are searching for opportunities to make money on their own without being dependent on a boss or being limited by their monthly salary. Trading is one of the ways. Trading currencies might be the best way!

Unfortunately for most, they come to the market led only by positive emotions and some mediocre strategies without any real discipline and stamina to succeed.

People need to learn to understand market and various conditions it may be in and how one can trade those. They should also learn when not to trade at all. Pro traders adhere to this rule very strictly.

In this Ebook you will learn how to identify specific market conditions and trade according to them. You will find out when you need to use specific technical indicators and when to avoid them. In the last chapter you will study how to trade support and resistance in combination with candle patterns.

Wish you good time and efficient learning!

Chapter 1

Understanding Market Conditions

One of the essential things that any trader who wants to become a pro has to know is that market conditions change. You may see some pair rising for a week, then jumping up and down at the same level for another week, then fall for a few days, after that rise for three days and then get choppy again. These things show the dynamics of currency market and any other financial market. If you try to trade currencies based only trend trading conditions where currencies keep on rising or falling you will probably have nice profits when markets are trending, but lose most of it when they stop and start ranging or jumping up and down (getting choppy).

Flexibility is the character feature that will help you to spot market changes, adapt and make cash under any market conditions. Some traders wait only for trend and they miss a lot of opportunities that are there in a range. Some "market experts" will tell you that you should not trade currencies that are choppy. It is also not the true. I mean if you understand what happens and you know where to enter and exit your trades when currencies are choppy you can trade and make a lot of money. Why should you skip opportunities if you know how to use them? You don't have to.

In this chapter I want to go through different market conditions and see what you can expect to happen with currencies when they undergo them and also how one can take advantage of that and make profit trading in any market state. However, before you can learn how to use a specific strategy you need to learn to identify what you see in front of your eyes and only then how to use that to make money.

Let us look through each market state and see how you can use that state to make profits. The first market state is a trending market.

Trending market

Trending market is a state of a currency pair when it has a clear direction: up or down. An uptrend is identified by higher highs and higher lows and a downtrend is identified by lower highs and lower lows. When you look at the chart of these you will see it as a chart of peak and valleys. Traders like trending markets most as they are the easiest to trade. Below are 2 examples of gbp/usd pair: one showing uptrend in the pair and one downtrend.

You can spot the uptrend that started on the 8th of June and ended on the 18th of June, 2015. This was a two week rally up with higher highs and higher lows and a total of 700 pips move.

The chart below shows a short term downtrend that preceded the uptrend in the chart before. It started on the 22nd of May and finished on the 1st of June. It was a little bit shorter in terms of time, but still good one for those who trade trends as lower highs and lower lows can be clearly seen on the chart.

gbp/usd 2 hour chart (an uptrend with clear higher highs and higher lows)

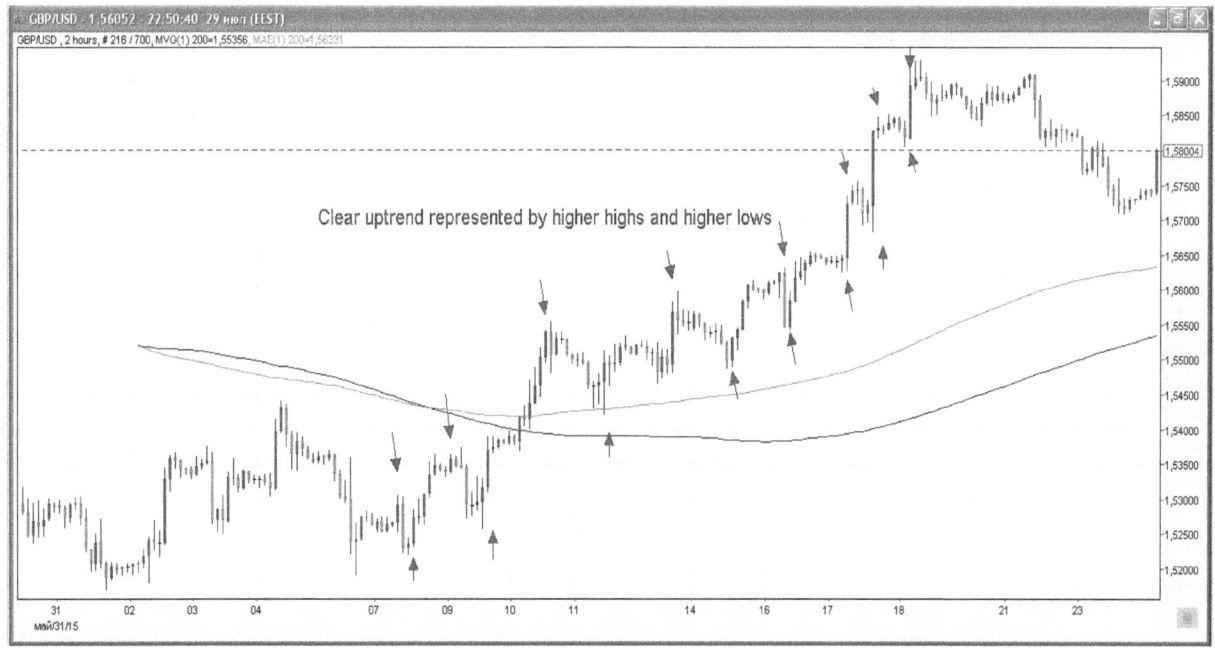

gbp/usd 1 hour chart (a downtrend with clear lower highs and lower lows)

How do you trade trending markets?

There is a common saying that is now regarded as an axiom and it is:"Buy on dips in an uptrend and sell rallies in a downtrend". This is probably the main way how you can trade trending markets, whether they go up or down.

Now if we look back again at 2 hour chart of gbp/usd that shows the pair is in an uptrend we can see those dips that are opportunities for those who want to go long the pair and join the move upwards. I marked six points where prices dip and consolidate. That's what you look for.

Firstly, you wait for a dip. When that happens you should expect somewhere between 1 to 4 hours of consolidation. When you see that price has stopped falling you wait and see whether it is not a temporary stop, but a permanent one. When that is confirmed (price does not make new lows) you can open a long order with some 30 pips below the lowest low in the dip.

Of course, when you buy during consolidation you won't probably buy at the lowest low, but you will be close to it. So, your stop loss order may be around 45-60 pips. But do not worry, when market is trending, you will get around 90-120 pips upwards on most days after a dip. So, your stop loss would be covered and profit will exceed your risk.

Remember, you need to see consolidation (some call it accumulation) period. That is the safest way to play. Do not rush to buy when prices are still falling. Pros call this process "catching of falling knives". You do not want to do that. You need to see that the fall is over. That's when you step in and start buying.

2 hour gbp/usd chart (consolidation areas are places where long orders should be opened)

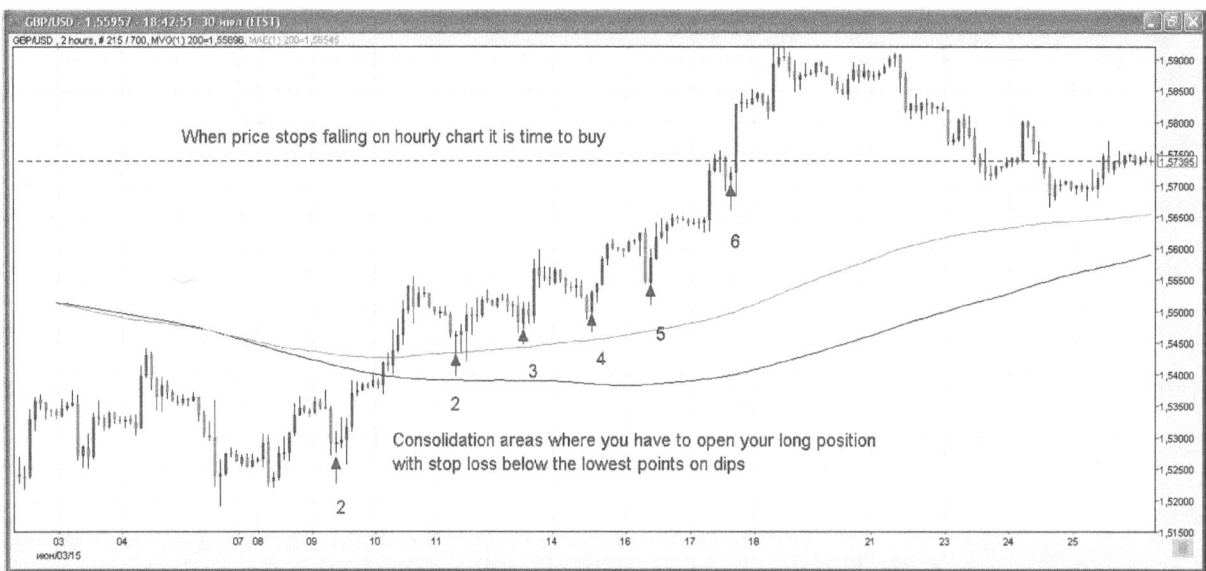

Below is another chart of gbp/usd that you have already seen one page above. It shows you the short term downtrend with classical rallies. I marked 5 points on the chart that show end of rallies where price stalls and stops rising. In most cases it consolidates from 1 to 4 hours and then the main downtrend continues.

When you see price stop rising on hourly chart and consolidating for a few hours you should initiate a short position with a stop loss of around 30 pips above the highest point of the most recent rally. As you most probably not catch the highest point in the rally, you will have a stop loss of around 45-60 pips.

Again, the move down on trending weeks will be 90-120 pips and those will exceed your risk level twice or even trice, so you will have excellent 2:1 or 3:1 risk/reward ratio.

Remember, you need to see consolidation (in a downtrend it is called distribution) period. That is the safest way to play. Do not rush to sell when prices are still rising. You need to see that the rise is over. That's when you step in and start selling.

2 hour gbp/usd chart (consolidation areas are places where short orders should be opened)

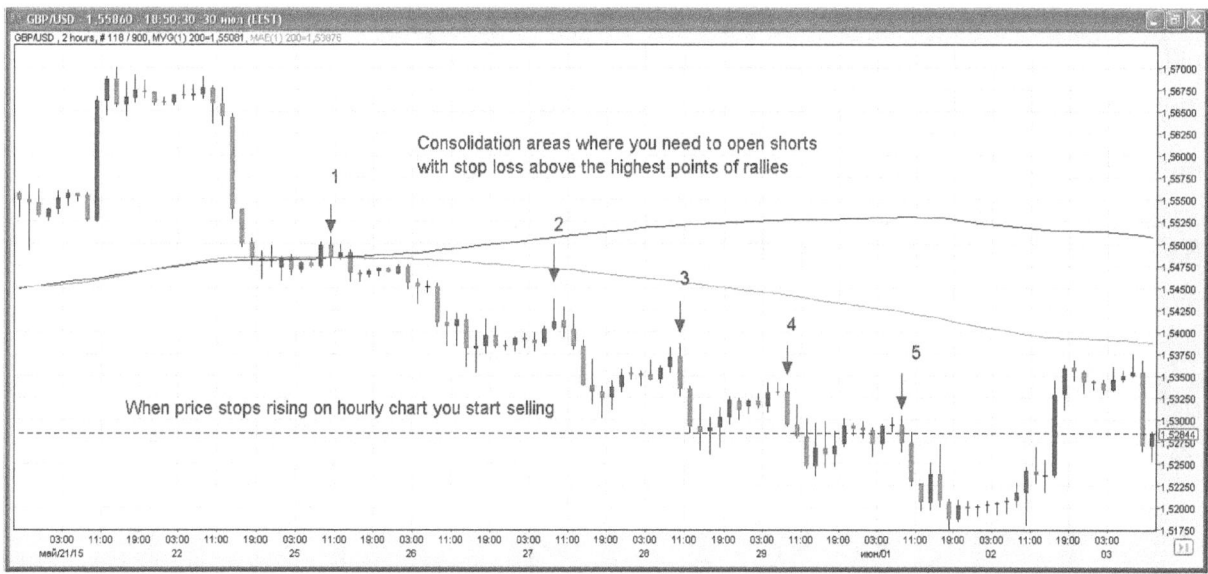

Ranging market conditions

It is no secret that most of the time currencies stay in ranges. It is safe to say that most currency pairs can be in a range ten months out of twelve. This may vary from year to year as some years see more trends than others, but general rule of thumb is to expect a ranging market through the year with a few months of trending conditions. Now, since most of the time market range we may want to find out what the specifics of a ranging market are and how one can trade it to make money.

You can easily identify a range when you see price fluctuating between two levels without breaching them. It means price goes up and meets a resistance level, which it cannot breach and then reverses. Then it goes to support level, which it cannot breach and then reverses again.

There are various ranges on different time frames, but in most cases a certain currency pair can stay within a limited range from one to five months and after the period a real breakout occurs and it starts trending. However, before that break occurs, price can visit those important support and resistance levels three, four or even ten times. There has to be some fundamental factor that would push price out of the boundaries of a given range and as long as that factor is absent a currency pair will keep on bouncing from those support and resistance levels.

A daily chart below shows you aud/usd pair from the 25th of July, 2013 to the 11th of April, 2014. It is a period of roughly 9.5 months. Within that period the currency pair fluctuated within a range of around 450 pips. 1.0600 level acted as strong resistance and 1.0150 as strong support. In the month of May, 2014 support was broken and a downtrend started.

However, you can see from the chart that price visited the above mentioned support and resistance levels quite a few times. Resistance of 1.0600 was visited 5 times and support of 1.0150 was visited 4 times. Every time the pair went to the resistance it was rejected and collapsed and every time it went to support it was rejected there and rose sharply. You could make nice cash by buying at support and closing your long position at resistance and reversing your trade by going short (selling) aud/usd at resistance and closing it somewhere near support.

aud/usd pair daily chart (support and resistance levels in a range)

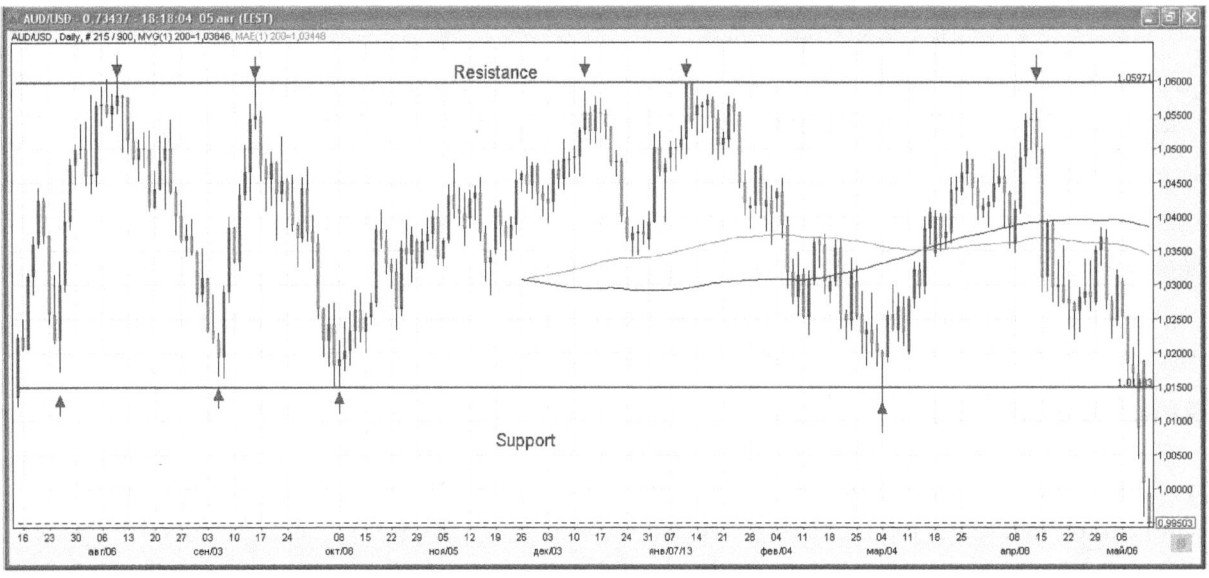

How to trade in a range

In the example above we look at a daily chart of aud/usd. We saw that during the period of about 9 months it fluctuated in a range of 450 pips. In the chart we saw that we had 9 situations where price came near important support and resistance levels and that gave us opportunities for reversal trades.

If we analyze closer price action around resistance level we will see that in some cases the level of 1.0600 was not reached and in a few instances in was exceeded. However, you will see that the biggest number of pips when currency pair missed 1.0600 level was 19 pips and the biggest number of pips when pair exceeded 1.0600 levels was 24 pips. It leads us to a conclusion that had we entered a short at 1.0570 with a stop loss at 1.0630 (60 pips stop loss) we wouldn't have missed a single short trade and wouldn't have had a single bad trade on the short side.

In each case we could have safely exited our short position 50 pips before our key support of 1.0150 level. This would have earned us 390 pips on each trade. The third and the fourth level of resistance were close to each other meaning that we would have taken 4 short trades instead of four, because the third one would still be opened when the fourth situation for shorting occurred.

The same can be said about support level. The price did not reach the level of 1.0150 on two occasions. However, the largest number of pips that the price missed the level was 23. The largest amount of pips that the currency exceeded the level was 37. So, we had four possibilities.

Had we used the same rule as in the case with shorting we would have gone long at 1.0180 with a stop loss at 1.0120. In one instance we would have incurred the loss (the price went up eventually and a stop loss of 70 pips would have saved us). We would have taken our profit 30 pips before key resistance of 1.0600 on three occasions. These three successful longs would have netted us 390 pips on each trade with a loss of 60 pips when our stop loss order was hit.

aud/usd daily chart (how to trade the range)

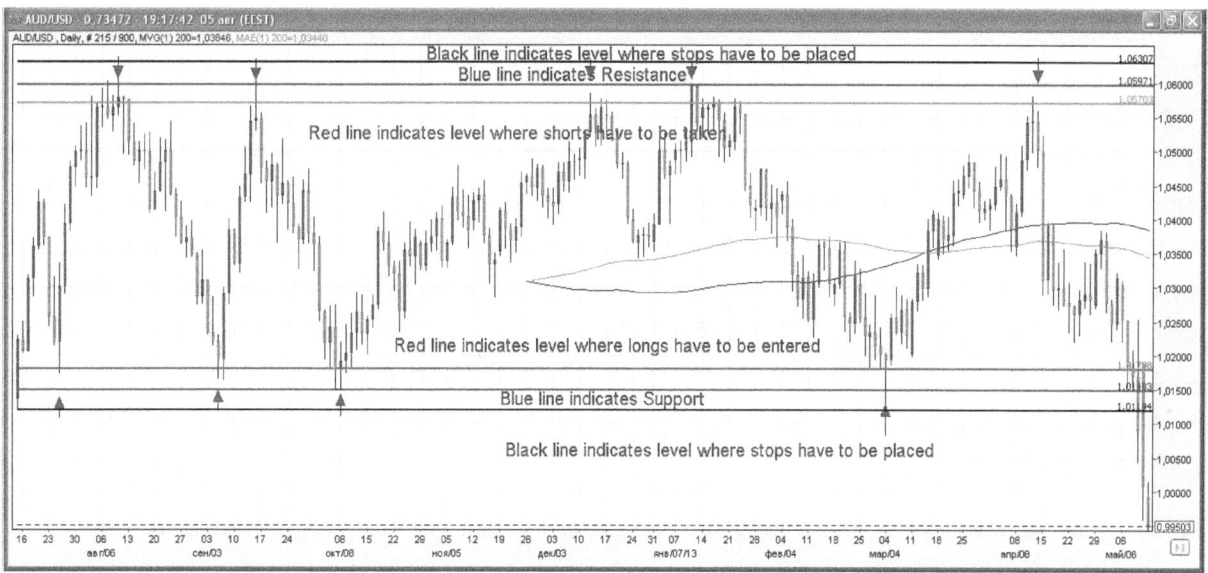

You can do a similar analysis on other currency pairs too. You have to remember that ranges can also last for a shorter period of time and in each instance you need to clearly identify correct support and resistance levels and trade with. If the range is smaller your stop loss and take profit orders will take smaller amount of pips too.

Choppy market conditions

Choppy market does not have clear direction and often not very clear support and resistance levels. When market is in this state for a specific pair you may see price jumping up and down, creating false breaks and basically going nowhere. It is a very difficult market to trade. However, there are some things you may notice happening in a choppy market and knowing those might also help you to make profits, despite the fact that the market is unpredictable for most traders. If you look at the example below with gbp/usd pair from the 28th of July to the 6th of August, 2015 you can see that the pair is moving sideways (choppy market), has no trend, nor clear support and resistance levels.

gbp/usd 1 hour chart (choppy market)

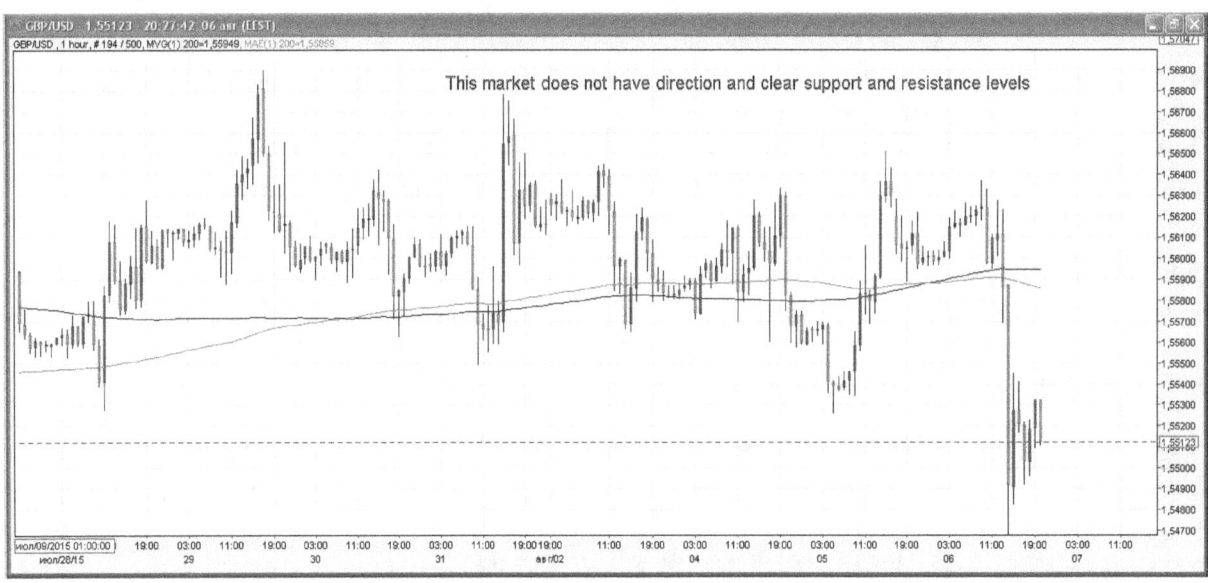

On the other hand, you can still trade this market if you notice some specific details about it. The chart below shows opportunities in a choppy market. Under these market conditions trading false breaks is the key, particularly trading against previous day's lows or highs. By this I mean when you see previous day's low broken you should be looking for opportunities to buy and when you see previous day's high broken you should be looking for opportunities to sell. In most cases you would be profitable, because very soon after a break occurs price often reverses and goes in the opposite direction.

In the example below you can actually see eight trading days. In these eight trading days you would have had six opportunities to trade either shorting when price broke previous day's highs or going long when price broke previous day's lows. There were four opportunities to buy and two opportunities to sell in these eight days. Depending on how you entered, where your stop loss was and where you exited you could have actually made money on all six trades without having any losses.

gbp/usd 1 hour chart (false breaks of previous day's lows or highs)

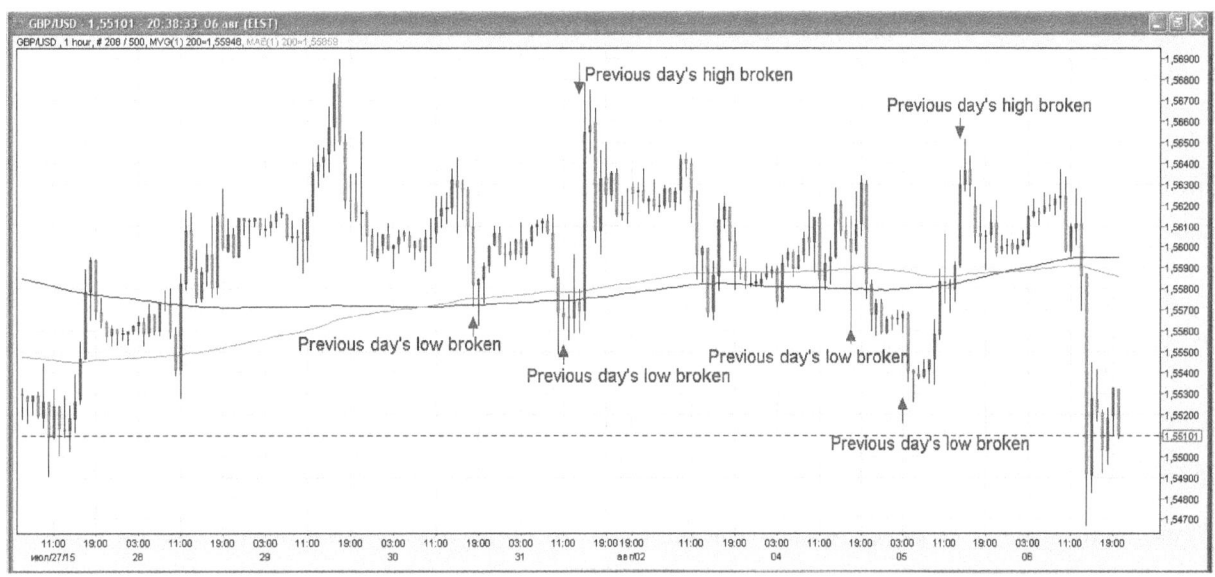

How to trade the choppy market

Having studies the example above we may conclude that the best way to trade a choppy market is to buy below previous day's lows and to sell above previous day's highs. But how do we enter hour orders, where exactly to we execute our orders. A thorough analysis shows that the best way to open trades in this market is by following 1 hour candles. When market breaks previous day's lows we place buy orders above 1 hour candle (1 to 3 pips above the candle). If market keeps on going down we move our orders and place it above the next hourly candle (1 to 3 pips above next candle). The stop loss has to go 3-5 pips below the lowest point of the day at that point.

The same is true about sell orders. When market breaks previous day's highs we place sell orders below 1 hour candle (1 to 3 pips below the candle). If market keeps on going up we move our orders and place it below the next hourly candle (1 to 3 pips below next candle). The stop loss has to go 3-5 pips above the highest point of the day at that point.

You may analyze how that works by studying the chart below. The first example for entering buy orders happened on the 30th of June, 2015 at 16.00 GMT. You may see that at 15.00 GMT price broke previous day's lows (of 29th of June). Next hour price went down, but then rallied. The high of that candle was at 1.5585, that's where the buy order had to be entered (1-3 pips) above the number. The low of the day (at that point) was 1.5562. That's where stop loss order had to be entered (3-5 pips below the point).

You can see that price went up for the rest of the day. Not much, but still up. You can trail your stop as market went up and close your trade with some 30 pips of profit before another day started (if you day trade you close your positions before new day starts or when New York market closes).

You can see that the next day was much better when market dipped lower below the low of previous day. You had to follow the same rule. You can see that on the 31st of July you would have made around 100 pips if you followed the rule for entering orders according to choppy market trading conditions.

A sell signal emerged the same day (31st of July) when price broke previous day's highs. Single candle closed at around 13.00 GMT You can see how price rallies strongly at about 11.00 and 12.00 GMT and then around 13.00 GMT previous day's high was broken and market started reversing.

You had to place a sell order below the low of the last hourly candle and that was the level of 1.5644 (1-3 pips below it) and a stop loss order above the highest point of the day, which at that point was 1.5675 (3-5 pips above it). As market went down, your sell order would have been opened and you could have netted around 30-40 pips had you exited your trade at around even number of 1.5600 (big market sharks close their trades around even numbers). Had you waited for the end of the day you would have got around 15-20 pips of profit as market slightly reversed before closing.

gbp/usd 1 hour chart (where to buy and where to sell)

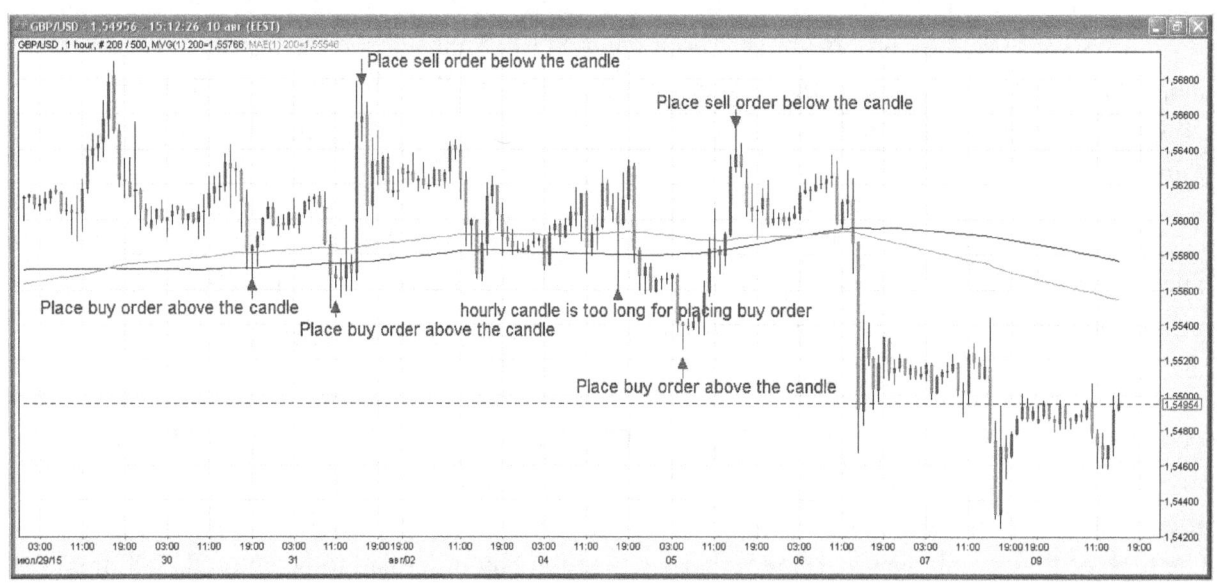

Chapter 2

Various market cycles and how to use them to make money

It would be difficult to understand Forex market and how it functions if you do not understand that market always goes in some kind of cycles: long term, intermediate and short term. You will always see trends, consolidations, accumulations, distributions and so on and so forth. You will also see trends that last for a few years, counter trends within those years (that may last from a few months to a year), monthly, weekly, daily and even intra day trends.

It is good if you learn to see big picture, intermediate size picture and finally current (micro) picture. You may look far in the distance if you know how to understand big (long term) market trends and then search for opportunities how to make profits on what you see on short term trend. Understanding both long term trends and short term trend complement each other and help you to become a better trader.

I understand that some people maybe long sighted or short sighted from birth or their sight develops one way or another as they grow old. It is also true about spotting market trends; some see big market moves, but fail to notice intermediate or short term ones. Others are good in spotting short term moves, but they do not see the big picture. I do believe that "trader's sight" can be developed and trained. It takes time and patience, but if you set a goal to learn to see market moves of various lengths and sizes in advance one day you will become proficient in that.

Long term moves (mega cycles)

Long term moves or cycles last from a year to decades. If you look at eur/usd monthly chart below you can see these long term moves. The shortest one was 5 months and the longest one 6 years. When you spot a cycle beginning it is obvious you have to trade in the direction of that specific long term cycle.

In fact, in most cases if you are able to grab a top when market turns bearish or a bottom when it turns bullish you can keep your position for a year or more and close it only when you see situation changing and a new cycle developing. This may not be easy task, but an achievable one. It takes years of practice, chart vision development and ability to interpret what you see on various time frames of a given chart.

If after a year of rise you see price failing to break resistance five or more times, it could be a good indication that the uptrend has exhausted itself and a downtrend is on its way. If after a year of falling you see price failing to break key support five or more times, it could be a good indication that the downtrend has exhausted itself and an uptrend is on its way.

Example of mega cycles

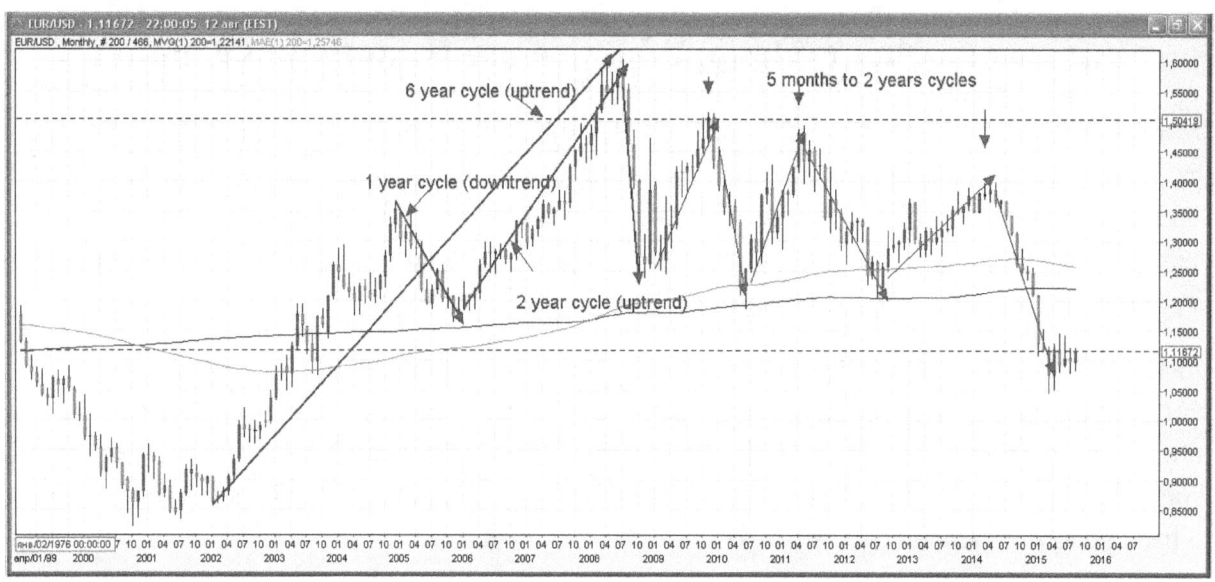

Trading mega cycles

I understand that not everyone is willing to wait for months for a signal and then enter the market and wait for a year before closing a position. However, there are advantages to such kind of trading. You do not have to sit glued to your computer screen every day. One time per week will be enough to look at your favorite currency pair to see whether a reversal is approaching or not. The same can be said about keeping your position.

You do not need to worry about daily fluctuations. You want to see something major happening and that can only be seen after weekly candle closes. Therefore, we would search for clues about taking a trade in a mega cycle on a weekly chart.

One good way to look for reversal signals is to wait for bearish pin or bullish pin candles to form on a weekly chart. In an uptrend you would have to be alert when you see a bearish pin form on a weekly chart and in a downtrend you would wait for bullish pin to form to start contemplating taking a long position.

I would look for a new high to be made in an uptrend and then a bearish pin to form. That would tell me that uptrend momentum is stalling and price may reverse any time. I would then place a sell stop position below the low of bearish pin and a stop loss order above the candle (some 10 pips).

A stop loss will be hit from time to time, but when market finally reverses you have a chance of making over 1000 pips. So, you would lose around 200-250 pips. In the example below you see that the first trade when bearish candle formed was a losing one. You would have lost around 250 pips. Of course, had you placed your stop loss at breakeven when price moved down for a couple of weeks you would have been breakeven on that trade. The second trade was profitable right from the start. Even if you had placed your stop loss at breakeven it wouldn't have been hit and you would have made around 3000 pips. You would have kept your position around 11 months before signs of a reversal upwards appeared.

Weekly chart of eur/usd (Two bearish pins indicate an upcoming reversal)

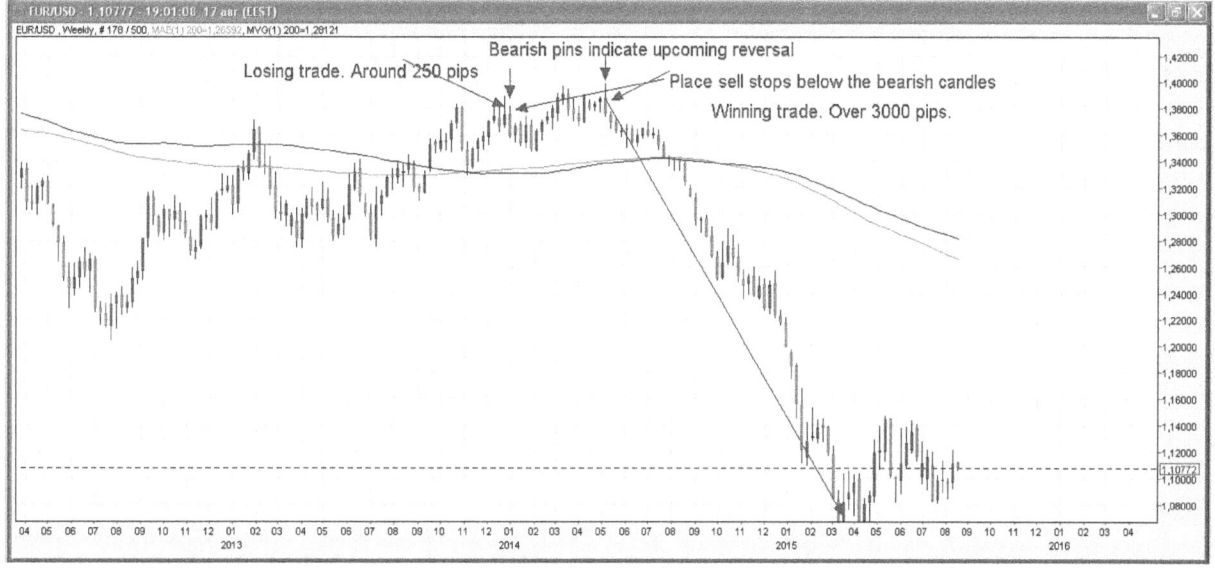

Weekly cycles

Weekly cycles are important for swing traders. These may last from a couple of days to a couple of weeks. Pro traders often talk about three day cycle in currencies. Large banks that offer liquidity to market participants often drive a currency pair in one direction for about three days and then reverse the move.

So, if you catch this weekly cycle and enter at exact top (with a short) or exact bottom (with a long) you can make hundreds of pips every week, provided you trade a number of currency pairs. Of course, exact three day cycles do not happen that often. In some cases you may see two day cycle, four day cycle or a full week (5 day) cycle.

However, directional moves that happen for a few days are quite often in currencies and you should pay attention to those. In the example below you see a three day move upwards that was preceded by two day sharp move downwards. And before those five days there was a period of some choppy price action, which was also tradable.

The best thing is that you can actually spot those trades and trade in the direction of a weekly cycle.

How to spot a weekly cycle?

There aren't exact rules, but there are some general guidelines and in most cases they work. You will experience losses by trying to identify and trade them, but when you become a sharp analyst you will also become a sharp trader that has very few losses and a lot of good trades.

2 day downward cycle and 3 day upward cycle in gbp/usd pair

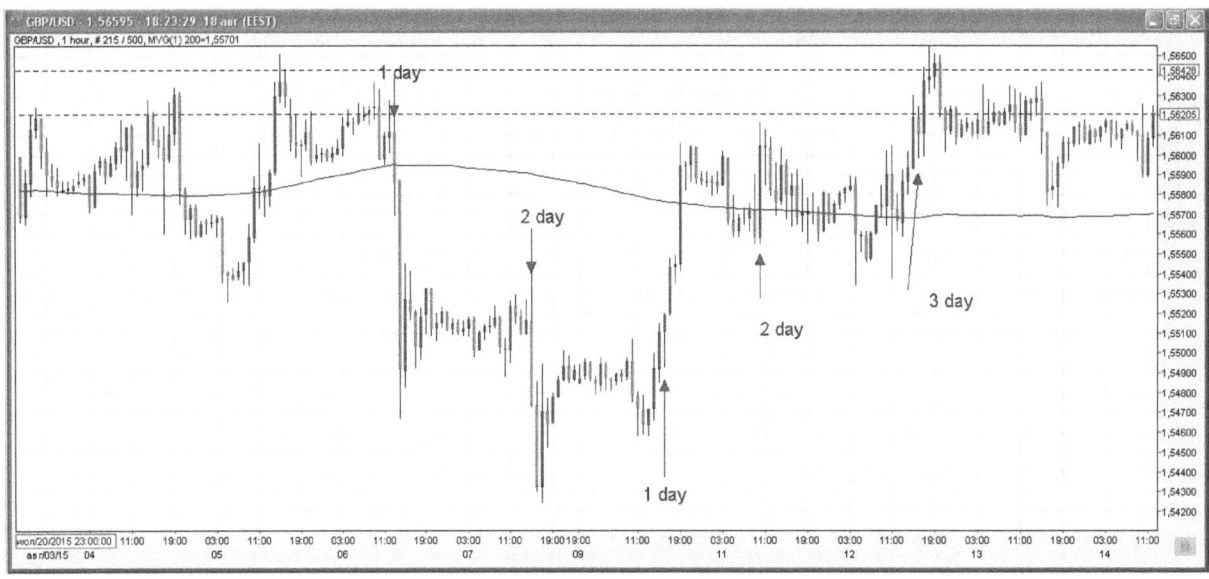

Firstly, before a trading week starts on Sunday evening you need to look through what happened previous week and how a specific currency (the one you intend to trade) closed on Friday. You need to see whether there was a week of directional move or price action was choppy.

In most cases, if the week was directional you will see some profit taking by the end of the week, sometimes on Thursdays or in most cases on Fridays. Then, on Mondays you can expect a reversal and a move in the opposite direction than previous week.

Previous example proves that. You can see how gbp/usd went down on Thursday and Friday (6-7 of August) and then on Monday reversed and went up for the rest of the week before reversing next Monday.

In this type of situations you will probably see some profit taking by the end of the week. Then, on Monday you can see some choppy price action when European session begins, in most cases price going in the opposite direction before reversing in the direction it will head later through the week or next couple of days.

That's what we saw on the 10th of August (Monday) when after going down for two days price reversed on Monday. In the early European session it broke above Asian highs, then reversed and broke below Asian session lows. Do not be surprised with this price action. It often happens and catches a lot of breakout traders by surprise.

Finally price consolidated below the low of Asian lows and started rising. It rose throughout the whole week before profit taking took place during European session on Friday.

You can see on the chart the area near 1 day three candles that clearly show prices consolidating after a drop. That was your signal to enter a long position in gbp/usd. An arrow points to exact candle where you needed to buy. Actually there were a number of possibilities to enter the market.

You could place a buy above any hourly candle that formed the low of Asian range. So, you could have had 3 possible long entries: 1.5481, 1.5478 and 1.5471. Of course, the last entry would have got you the best possible price, but the other two were good too. Your stop loss order had to be 3-5 pips below the lowest point of that day (at about 1.5455-53).

Entry level for gbp/usd reversal trade on Monday

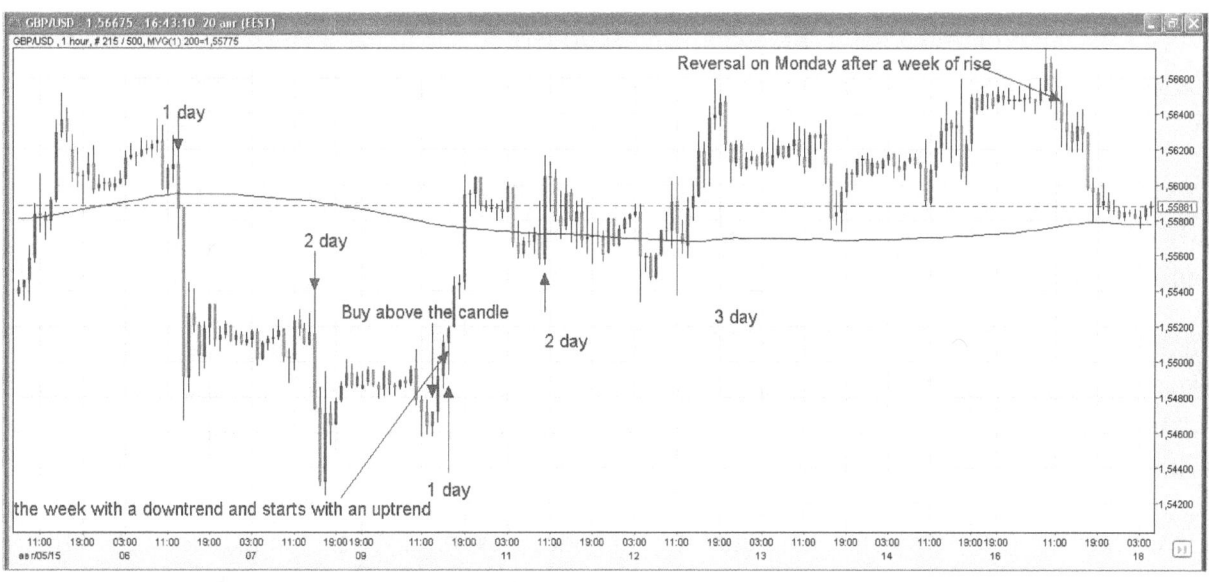

You should also remember that a reversal can take place any day of the week, not necessarily Monday. You will sometimes see it on Tuesday or the end of the week on Thursday if the swing move is very strong.

Another thing to remember is that if a very strong trend develops you simply have to trade in the direction of the prevailing trend and not wait for reversals, because those are very rare and you will not make much money trading counter trend moves.

When a market settles back into range you can trade in both directions much better than you can do that in a trending environment. Again, do not forget that trends are not that often guests in financial markets. They do come and go and prices fall back into their ranges.

Learn to watch cycles, particularly weekly to take advantage of reversals that take place once in 3 or 5 days. You can make hundreds of pips in multiple currency pairs. Of course, you would start by simply looking at the chart every weekend and analyzing what happened during the week with your favorite pair or a couple of pairs. Try to spot when market turned, when it formed peak or bottom, which day of the week it reversed and how it did that.

When you feel you are good at analyzing, try to trade bit by bit. You may start with a demo account that any Forex broker will provide you with. Or you can open a mini real account and trade risking very small amounts till you feel comfortable and can take bigger risks and trading bigger positions (consequently making bigger profits too).

Daily cycles

Day traders will most likely search for opportunities to open and close trades during 24 hours. A lot of people lose money day trading. They either use too many strategies or they do not follow their trading signals, or they simply trade the wrong way.

One of the best ways to day trade is to define a short term cycle a market is in and trade only in the direction of prevailing direction of that cycle. If the tendency is down you only wait for opportunities to short (sell). If it is up you only wait for opportunities to go long (buy).

I have used the same chart of gbp/usd 5 day bullish cycle to illustrate how one can take advantage of short term daily opportunities to trade in the direction of prevailing trend. In a bullish market you would wait for market to go down before you buy.

In most cases you would want it to go below Asian lows, form a reversal pattern and then you buy. Alternatively, you can simply place buy orders above hourly candle highs and move them till your order is opened. The stop should always be below the lowest point of the day (at that point).

On each of the five days you had a possibility to go long every day. The second day wasn't that good, but all the others would have netted you nice profit. Even on the second day you could have got some profit, if you watched what happened on 15 minute chart and having seen signs of reversal exited the market.

Not all trades work out. You must be aware of that and do not buy into some scams that tell you otherwise. You will experience losses and you may have a lot of them before you learn to select the best trades, spot market conditions, avoid overtrading and etc.

You see, there might not be a clear cycle in the market and market can simply be choppy for a number of weeks and it will be difficult for you to trade. It may go up one day and down another. This happens quite often. If you are not able to spot reversals in those periods, it is better not to trade at all till situation clears up and market starts going in some direction.

You can become impatient at such times, but waiting is only for your benefit. Do not rush trading if you don't understand what is happening. You will only get hurt. Of course, you can learn a lot from the pain of losing, but too much pain will get you disappointed and you can quite trading before you can actually start seeing any positive results.

Entry points for day trading gbp/usd

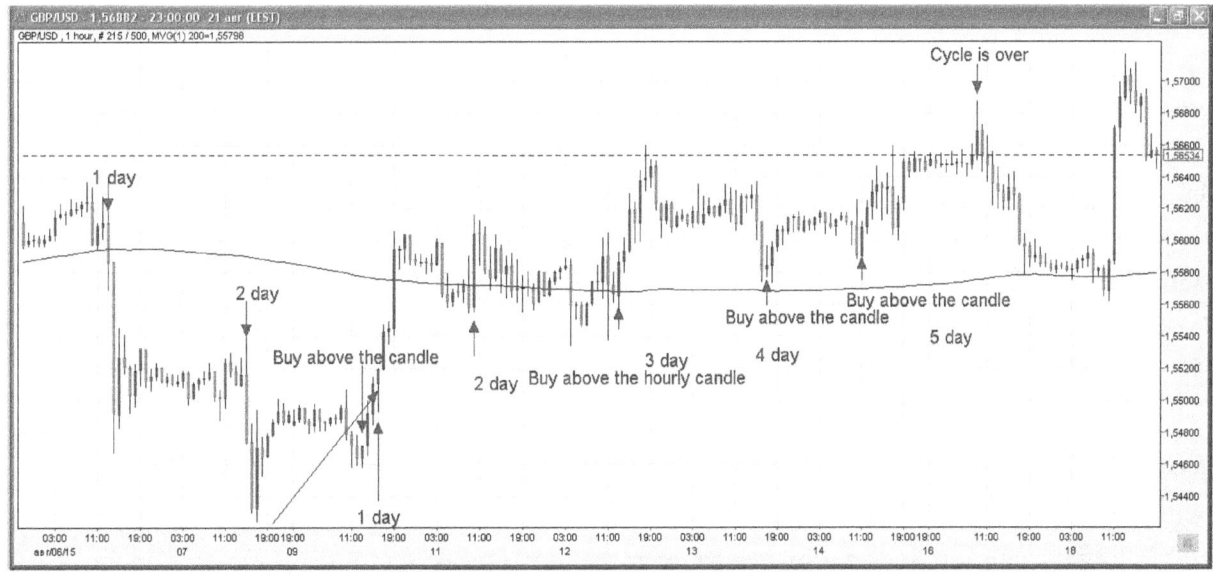

Chapter 3

Follow the Leader: Choosing the Best Currency Pairs and Leaving Laggards Behind

The name of the chapter may sound somewhat funny to you, but it actually means what it says: you have to follow the leader among currency pairs and avoid holding a laggard. The concept may be new to you, but those who follow a lot of financial instruments will surely know what I am talking about. A legendary trader introduced this concept around 100 years ago. He knew that stocks and commodities tend to stay in ranges for some time, but eventually they break out and start trending. He also noticed that those securities that break out first out of their bases and ranges tend to perform better than those that lag behind. Therefore, he made a conclusion that it is better to buy only a few stocks that break from their bases first and leave the other laggards behind.

The same is true with currencies. If you notice that most currencies are in a range you need to wait for the range to be broken and then you need to see which currency pair or pairs does it first and follow it (them). It does not matter whether the move turns out to be upwards or downwards, because in currencies you can make money just as successfully shorting (selling) currency pairs as going long in them (buying).

I want to give you a few examples of currencies and you can decide for yourself which ones you should have bought and held for a longer period of time. The first batch of examples is with US dollar denominated currencies.

Breakout in eur/usd

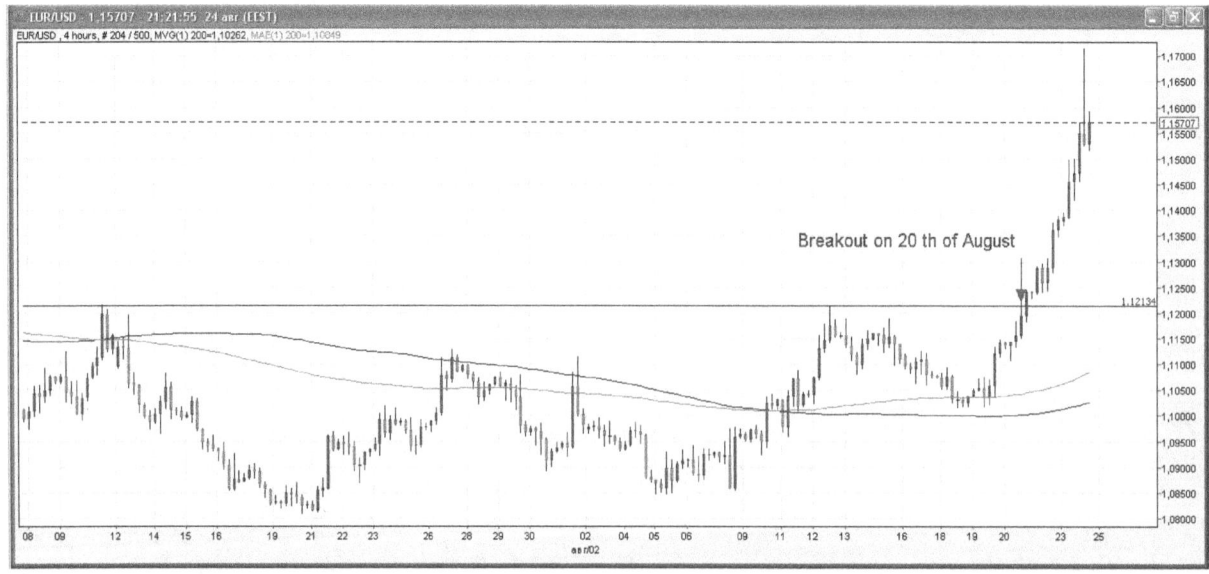

Breakout in gbp/usd

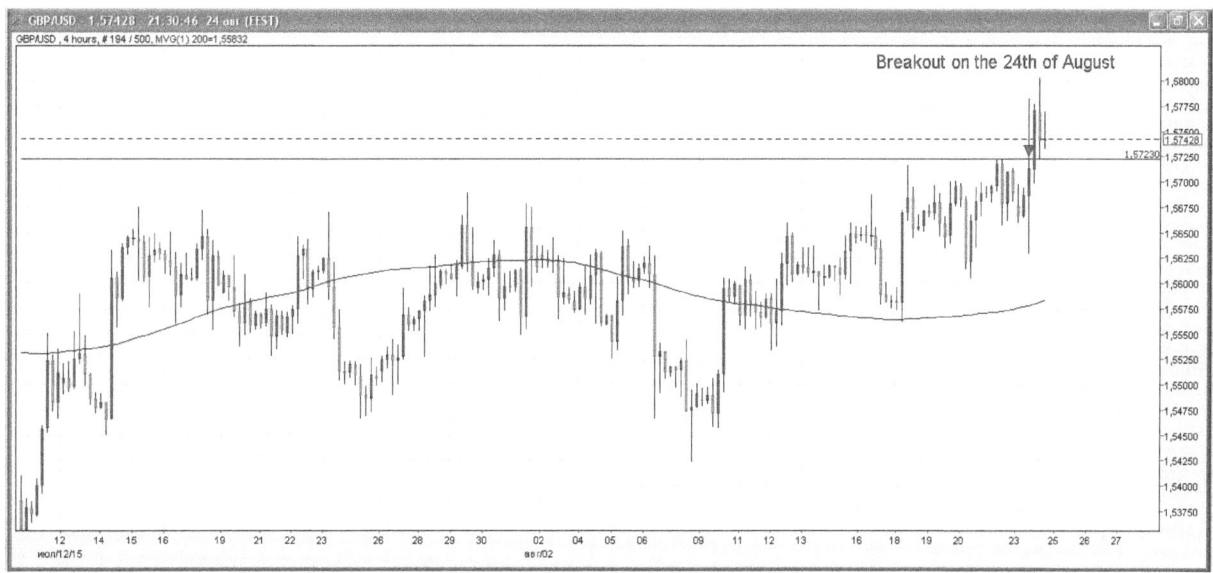

Breakout in usd/jpy

I can take other pairs that are USD denominated, but in others, such as aud/usd, nzd/usd or usd/cad US dollar actually rose. This is also very useful information that can help us to single out the weakest and the strongest currency pairs for trading. If by looking at the charts we define that eur/usd and usd/jpy were the strongest, because both of them broke out on the 20th of August, 2015, we had to be in those pairs and keep selling US dollar.

Here is what happened with other major currencies against US dollar.

Breakout in usd/cad (US dollar rises against Canadian dollar)

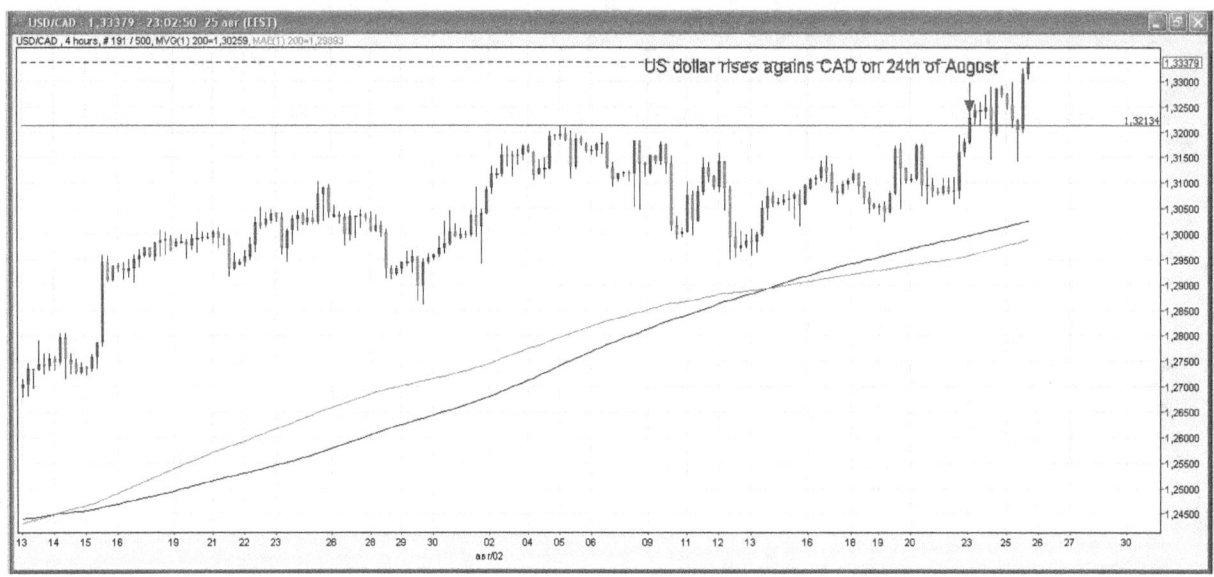

Breakout in aud/usd (US dollar rises against Australian dollar)

Breakout in nzd/usd (New Zealand dollar falls against US dollar, but quickly comes back into previous range)

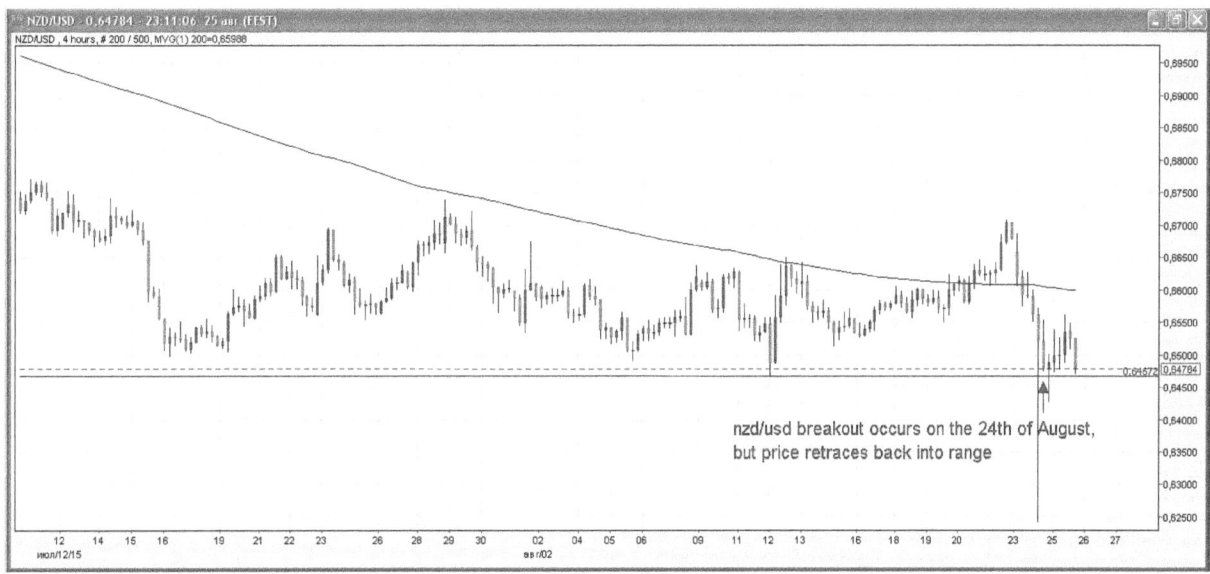

The examples show that the best plan of action in these situations was to sell usd/jpy on the 20th of August, when the pair broke 123.70 level or (and) buy eur/usd pair on the 20th of August when the pair broke 1.1200 level. Now, knowing the fact Japanese Yen was the strongest against US dollar, but US dollar at the same time moved up against Canadian dollar, Australian dollar and New Zealand dollar we may have also traded by selling Australian dollar, Canadian dollar and New Zealand dollar against Japanese Yen.

Let's look at what happened on the above mentioned Yen pairs and how you could have profited from that.

Breakout downwards in aud/jpy

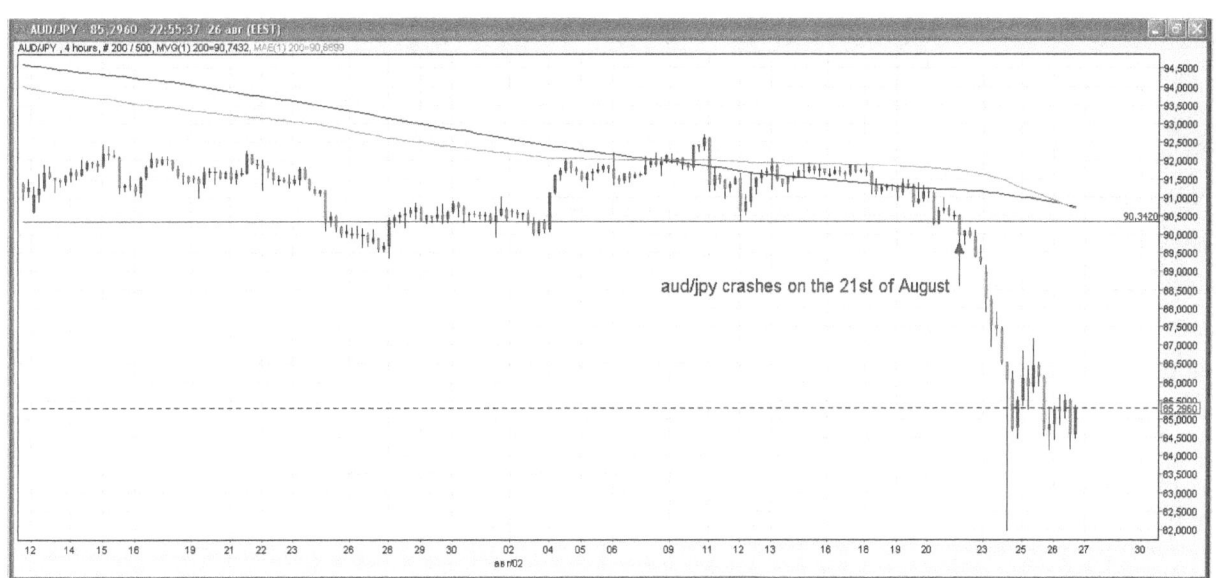

Breakout in cad/jpy downwards on the 21st of August

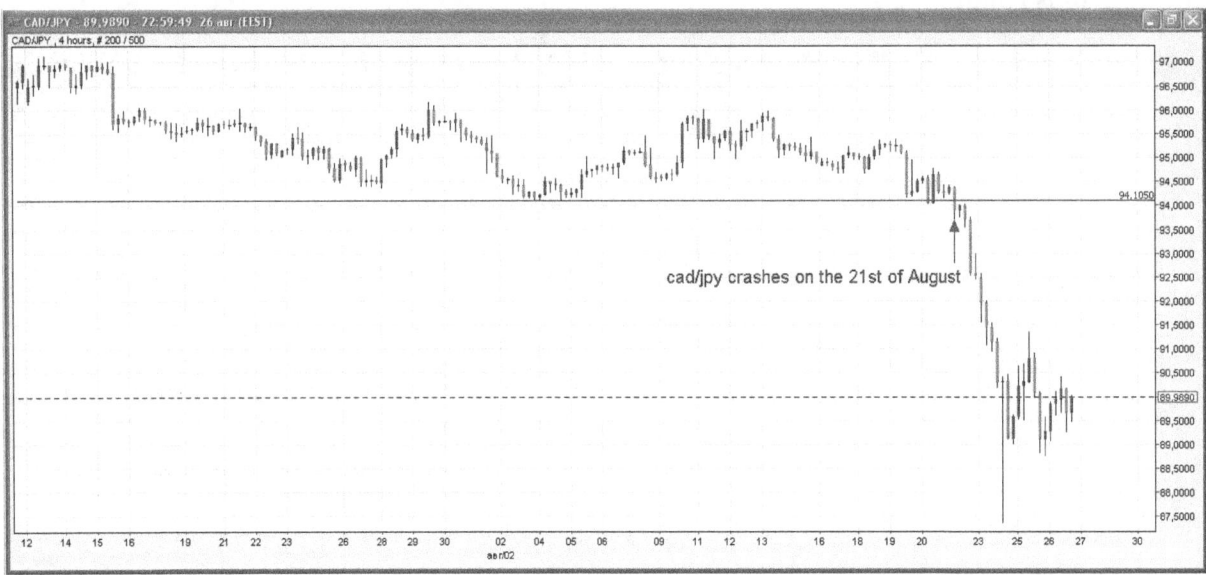

Breakout in nzd/jpy downwards on the 21st of August

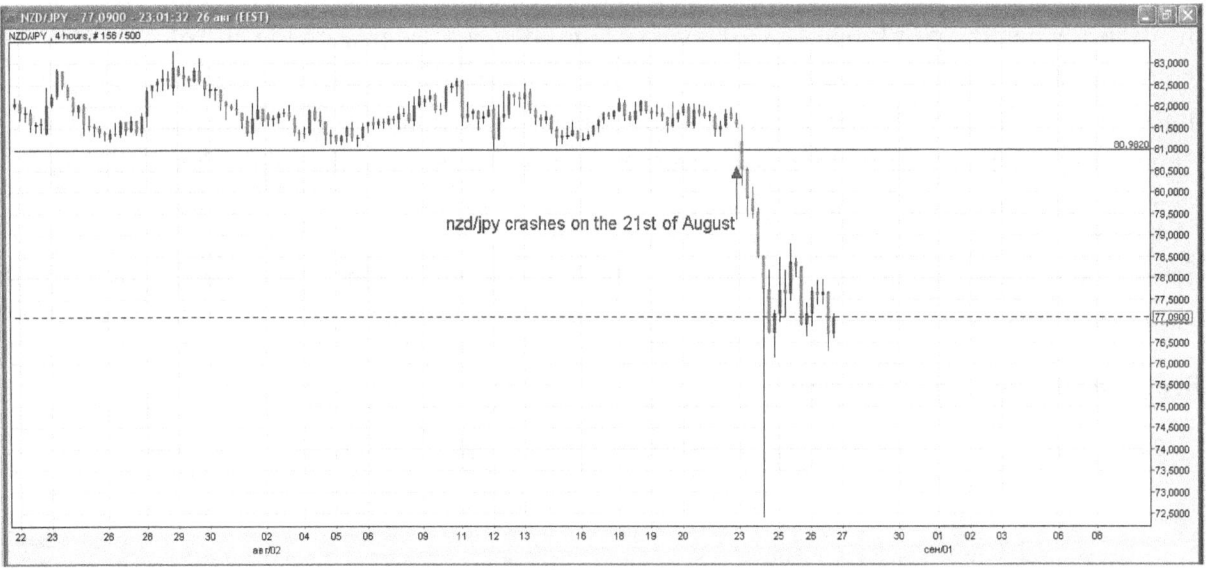

Now you can see that you could have taken a short position in any of Yen denominated pairs that have been presented in the examples above: aud/jpy, cad/jpy and nzd/jpy. All of them broke down on the 21st of August and as you had already had nice profit in eur/usd and usd/jpy pair. You could have moved your stop loss into positive territory and opened extra positions in other Japanese crosses by buying Japanese Yen against commodity currencies: AUD, CAD, and NZD.

Now, we have also stated that Euro was the second strongest pair that rallied against US dollar, which means that we could have also traded Euro against Australian dollar, Canadian dollar and New Zealand dollar.

In that case you would have opened eur/aud, eur/cad and eur/nzd long (buy) positions. This choice could be a very good diversification for your portfolio as these Euro crosses often form nice and big trends which will enable you to make a lot of money.

Let's look at eur/nzd chart

Breakout in eur/nzd (pair breaks upwards on the 24ᵗʰ of August)

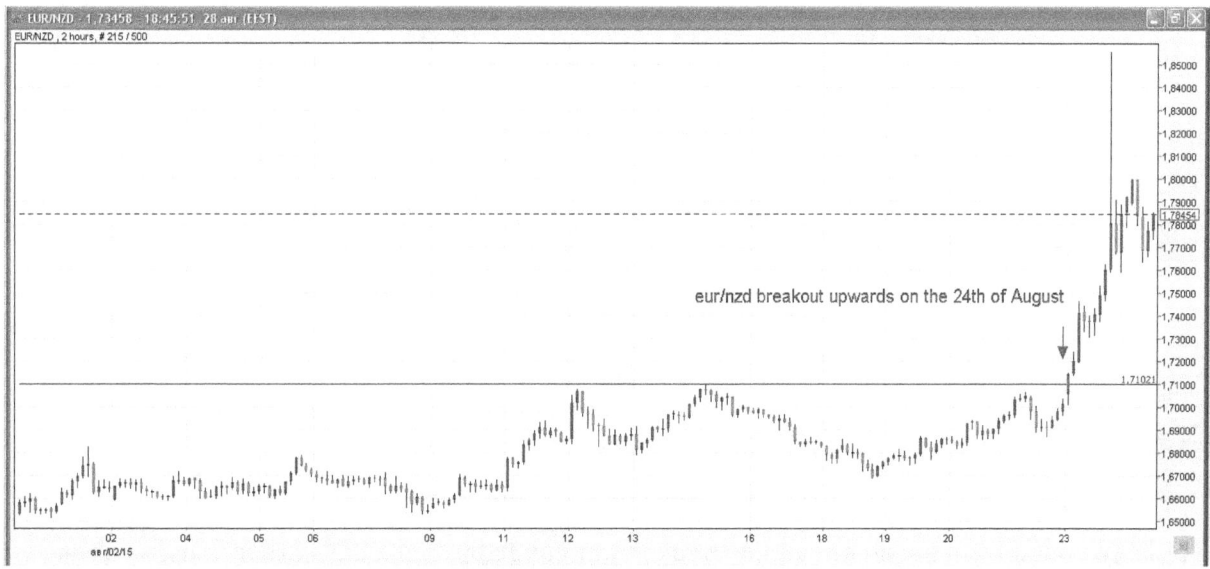

You can see that the move was really spectacular as eur/nzd moved around 1400 pips in one day before reversing sharply the same day. Anyway, you could still have got some 1000 pips had you traded a break upwards.

Breakout in eur/aud on the 21ˢᵗ of August

A very similar chart to the one before, except for the fact that eur/aud broke upwards earlier. The pair rallied around 1300 pips before reversing downwards. The move lasted just 2 days. I guess it was still worth it to trade it.

Breakout in eur/cad pair on the 20th of August

You may notice from the chart that the break in eur/cad happened a day earlier than in eur/aud and a few days earlier than in eur/nzd. The move upwards was around 950 pips, somewhat smaller than in the other two pairs. However, you would have made enough money on the pair and this breakout trade.

How to trade these moves

The best way to trade these moves, as you may understand is to buy or sell currency pairs when they break out of their ranges whether up or down. Let's look at a couple examples from the same currency pairs and the same charts, but with entry levels, stop loss area and take profit target zones.

If you look at eur/usd example below you see exact spot where you need to enter your long. The high of the range before the breakout occurred was at 1.1213. So, added a few pips and entered a buy stop at 1.1215 level with a stop below a breakout candle at 1.1150. So, the stop loss was 75 pips. Take profit should have been taken when a clear big bearish candle closed at 1.1530. So, you would have risked 75 pips, but actually gained 315 pips. Excellent risk/reward ratio of 1:4!

Entry, stop and take profit target on eur/usd long trade

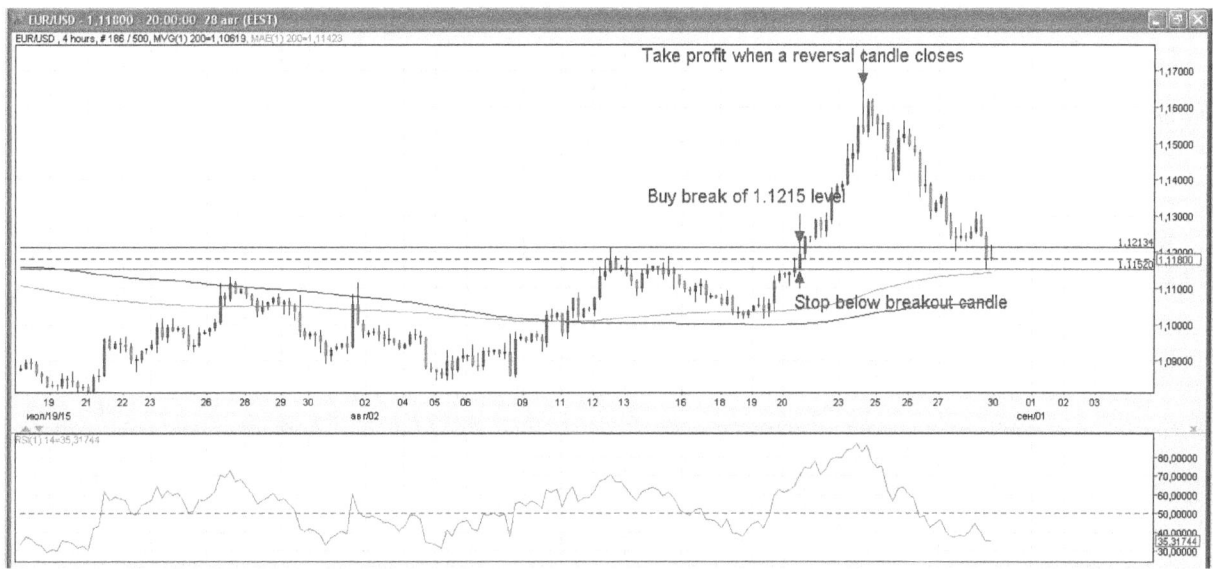

The second pair that broke early and performed very well was usd/jpy. In fact, it was the best pair out of all US dollar denominated pairs. So, let's see how you could have traded it. You had to enter a short position on the breakout of 123.65 level with a stop loss above breakout candle. It was at 123.94 (a few pips above it). So, the stop loss order was only 30 pips. That is really small taking into account that you entered an order for a large break downwards.

Take profit had to be taken when a large bullish candle closed 119.20. So, you would have made at least 445 pips. Of course, it was very far from the low of the day as we had a huge rally upwards when the pair hit 116.13 level, but it is not possible to grab every pip in every move. Be sure to grab most of the most and you will be a really good trader. In this case you would have exited 300 pips above the low of the move. Anyway, your risk reward ratio in this case would have been almost 1:15. Not bad, huh? So, forget those 300 pips, you had a super risk reward ratio and excellent profit.

Entry, stop and take profit target on usd/jpy short trade

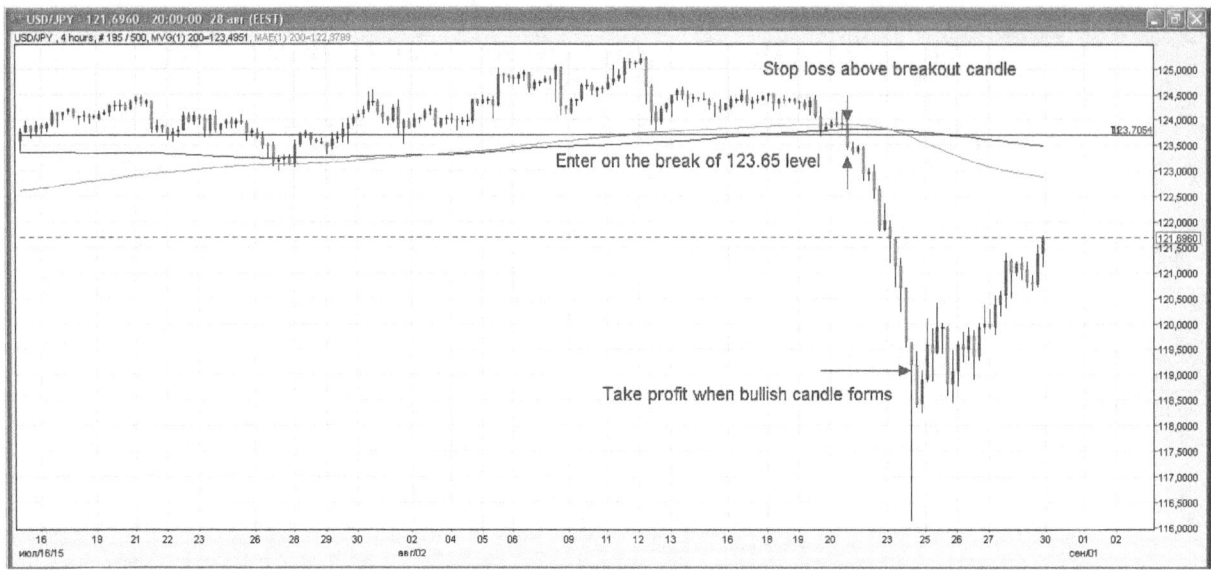

As Japanese Yen performed so well in these breakout trades, let's look at more examples of entries with Yen denominated pairs.

Let's start with aud/jpy.

As you remember the pair broke downwards on the 21st of August. The breakout level was 90.30. You simply had to enter a sell stop order below the level (maybe a few pips). Stop loss had to be placed a few pips above the breakout candle, which in our case was 90.55. Imagine, in this situation the stop loss order was only 25 pips. Some day traders use that type of stops, even bigger ones. Of course, you had to place a stop at that spot after the breakout candle closed. Initially it could be somewhere at 91.10. You need to move your stops too, when market moves in the direction you have anticipated.

You may spot a huge bullish candle on the 24th of August. That's where you had to take your profit and leave the market. So, you would have closed your short trade at 86.10. You would have made 420 pips. Again, your risk/reward ratio would have been around 1:17. That is incredible! You can lose a lot of times trading breakouts, but if you have this good risk reward ratio you will always be in profit.

Entry, stop and take profit target on aud/jpy short trade

Let's look at another Japanese Yen example: cad/jpy

This pair as aud/jpy pair discussed above broke the low of the range on the 21st of August. You had to enter a short position when 94.00 level was broken. Stop loss, as usually had to be placed above the breakout candle. In our case it had to be at 94.42 level. So, 42 pips stop loss is quite good again.

Take profit had to be locked in when huge bullish candle closed. In our case, it was 90.35. So, you would have made around 370 pips of profit on the trade. That is around 1:9 risk/reward ratio.

Entry, stop and take profit target on cad/jpy short trade

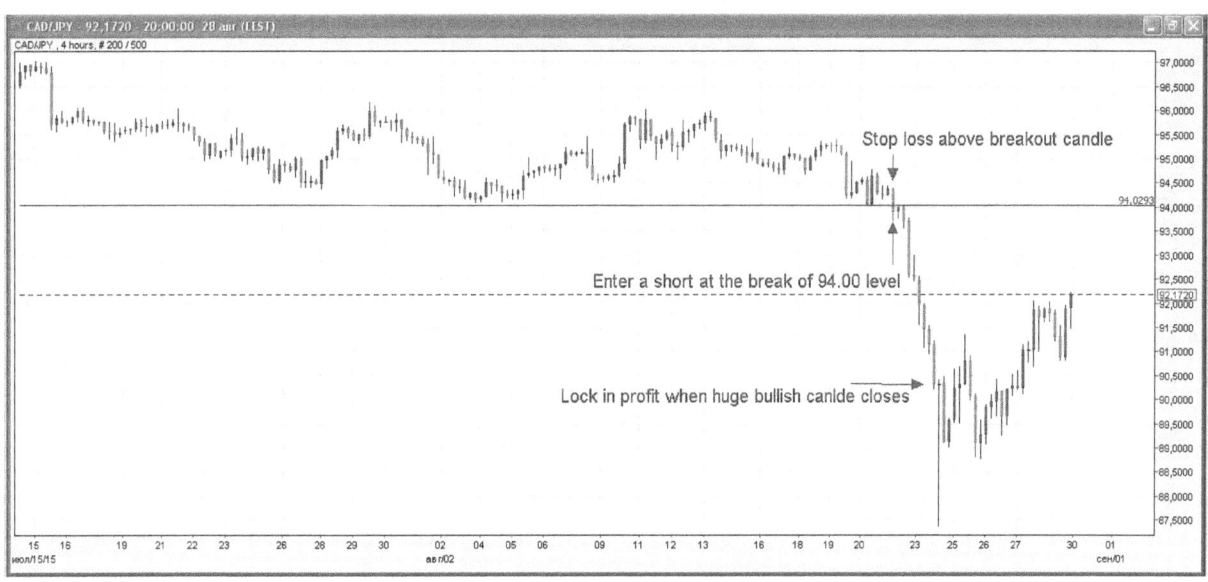

Our last example with Japanese Yen is nzd/jpy pair.

It was the last of Japanese pairs to break. The breakout occurred on the 24th of August and you had to enter a short at the break of 81.00 level. Stop loss had to be at 81.57 level.

Take profit had to be taken when huge bullish candle closed and it was at 77.73. So, you would have made 225 pips. It is obvious that you would have also left around 500 pips on the table. Well, you need some kind of rules for exiting and reversals are not always that dramatic. Of course, you could have sat by your pc all day and closed your trade at a much better level, but swing traders don't usually stay at their pc's all day.

Anyway, risk reward ratio in this case was around 1:4. It is still excellent risk/reward ratio and you should have taken a trade.

Entry, stop and take profit target on nzd/jpy short trade

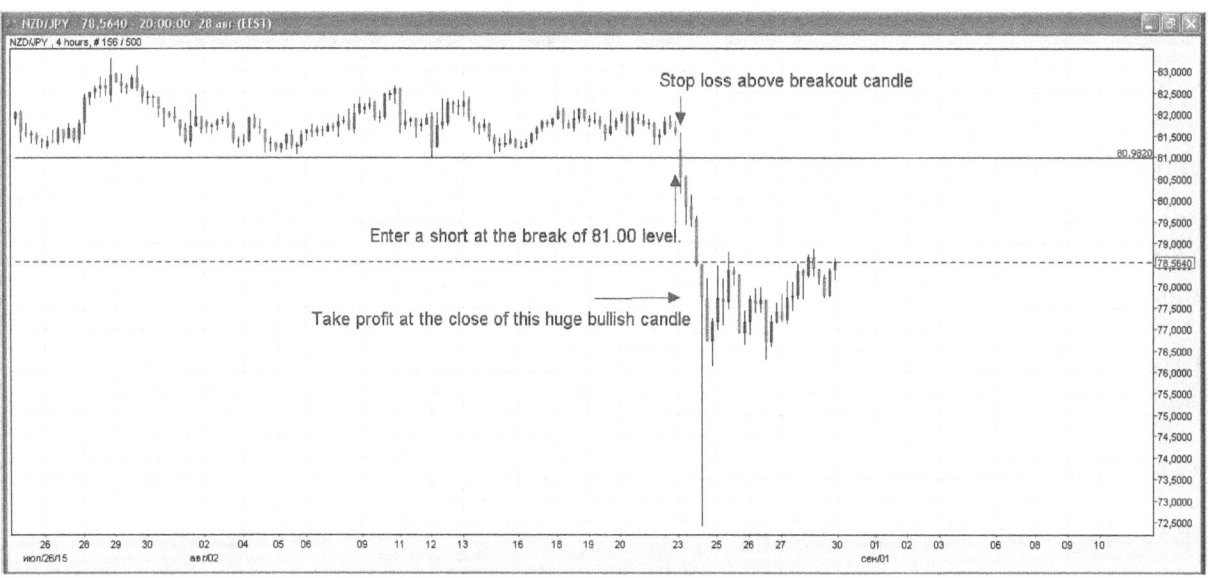

Ok, let's look at the last batch of trades you could have taken. This time with Euro as denominated currency in Euro crosses. If you remember from previous examples where breakout level and date was given, these rallied a lot in a matter of a few days.

So, eur/aud comes first.

We know that eur/aud broke upward channel of a range on the 21st of August. You had to place a buy stop position a few pips above 1.5300 level (when the level was broken upwards). Stop loss had to be placed below the breakout candle at 1.5225.

Take profit had to be taken when huge bearish candle closed. It was at 1.5965 level. Again, you would have left some 600 pips on the table, but when market collapses so fast you need to get out with what you have and do not regret about extra profit you have lost. All in all you would have still got 665 pips. That is close to 1:9 risk/reward ratio. That is still really good!

Entry, stop and take profit target on eur/aud long trade

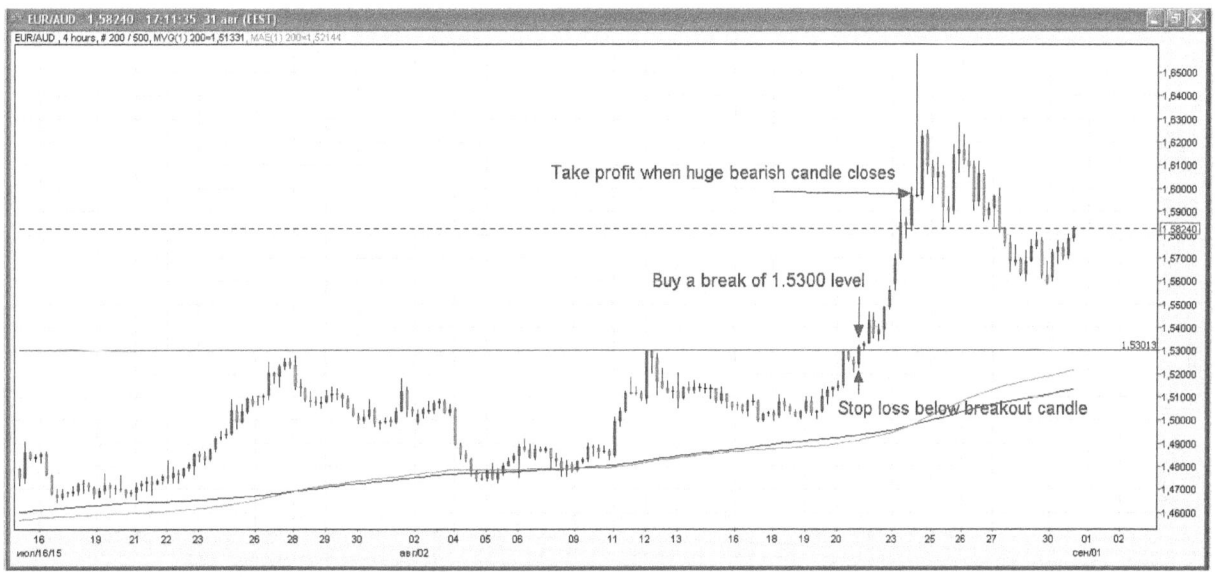

Let's look at another example.

This is how you should have traded eur/cad.

Euro broke up against Canadian dollar a day earlier than eur/aud (on the 20th of August). You had to place a buy stop order at 1.4615 level for a breakout and a stop loss order below the breakout candle at 1.4583. Price came very close to the level, but stop was not hit. 32 pip stop loss was excellent.

Take profit had to be taken when a huge bearish candle closed on 4 hour chart at 1.5210 level. You would have got 595 pips on the trade. That is about 1:18 risk/reward ratio. Could you ask for more? I seriously doubt it.

Entry, stop and take profit target on eur/cad long trade

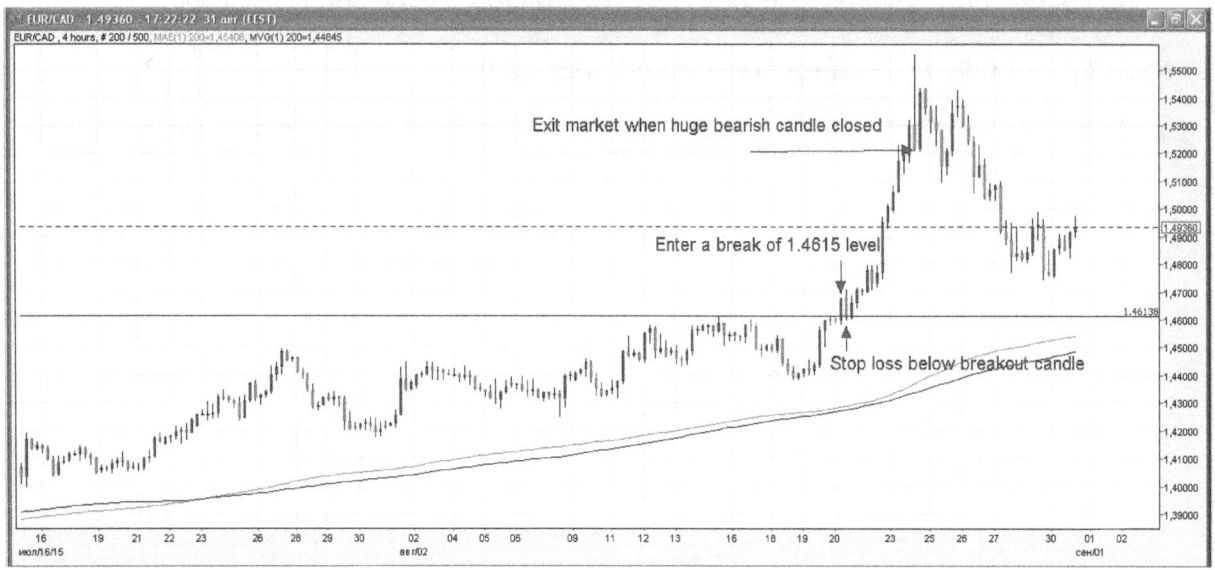

Let's go to our last Euro denominated pair – eur/nzd.

The pair broke out past key resistance level on the 24th of August, a few days later than eur/aud and eur/cad. But you would have still made nice cash had you entered a break of 1.7100 level. Stop loss had to be placed below the breakout candle of 1.7014.

Take profit, had to be taken when this huge bearish candle close. It was at 1.7804 level. It means you would have made around 700 pips on the trade. The same amount of pips would have been left on the table, but I will not repeat myself that it is inevitable in trading to leave a lot of profit on the table due to the fact that you do not know when the market is going to reverse exactly.

Risk/reward ratio was splendid again: 1:8. So, despite the fact you left a lot of pips on the table you would have made a lot of pips if you had made this breakout trade. Learn to concentrate on what you can do, not on what you cannot do.

Entry, stop and take profit target on eur/nzd long trade

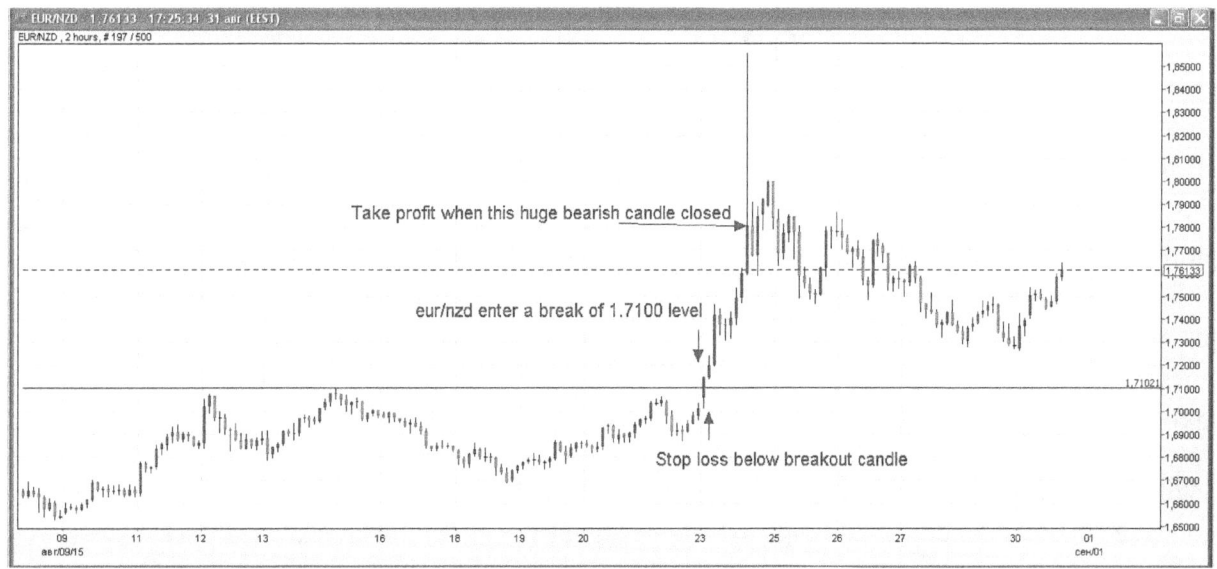

Chapter 4

Trading with Indicators: What to Use and When

A lot of pros simply reject usage of most indicators and some do not use any at all. The main reason for that is that most of them are lagging. The truth is that you may get a signal when the move is already over. Let's say you follow a signal of moving averages crossovers. It is a very simple system that gives a buy signal when a short term moving average (let's say 50) crosses long term average (let's say 200) up from below and a sell signal when a short term moving average crosses long term average down from above. However, if price is running fast you may miss a few hundred pips before the signal occurs and the move might be over when you actually take a position.

I will give you a few examples with crossovers in gbp/usd. The chart below shows that Pound collapsed against US dollar 200 pips before the signal was given by crossover of moving averages. You would have missed the bulk of the move despite the fact you would be in profit, because price continued going down after that.

Bearish crossover a signal to sell gbp/usd on hourly chart

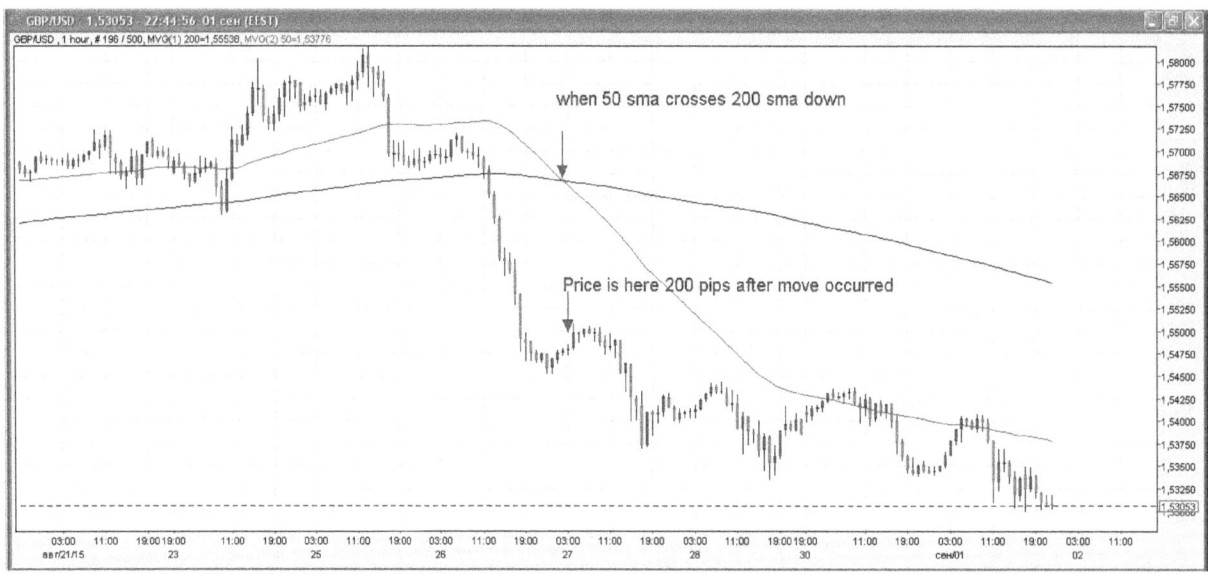

This is another example with gbp/usd crossover of moving averages. This time signal was given after price moved around 150 pips up. And the signal was given only after a few days after the move. By that time you can actually expect a top to form and momentum to be lost or slowed down.

Bullish crossover a signal to buy gbp/usd on hourly chart

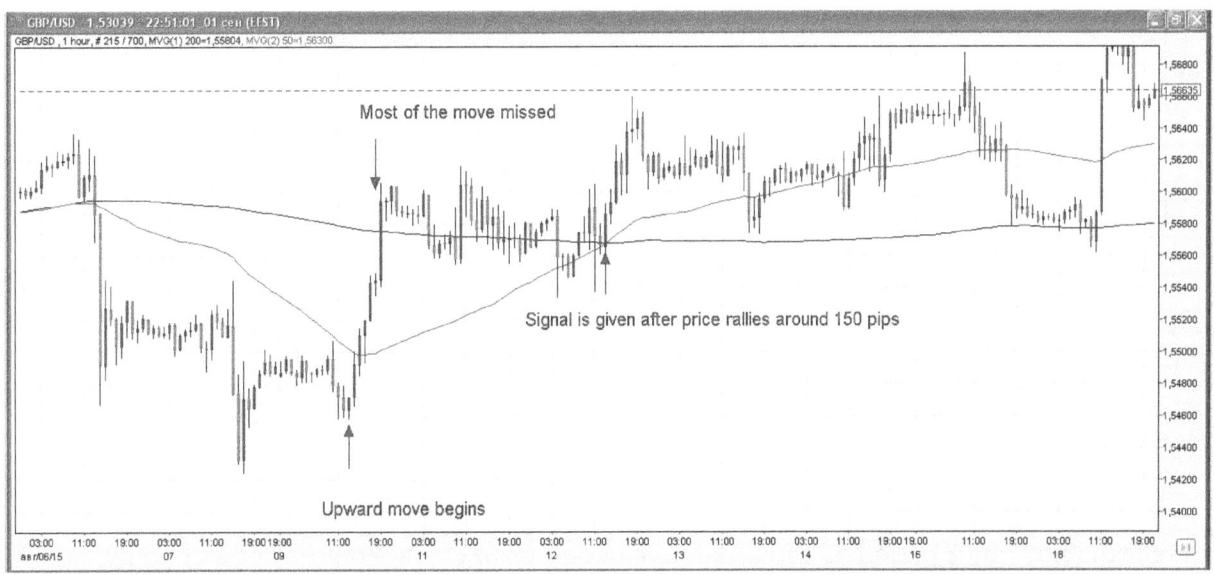

The same can be said about moving averages acting as support or resistance levels. If you try to trade by simply using a moving average to identify a support or resistance level you will have a lot of bad trades.

200 simple moving average is probably the most famous of all moving averages. And it works best. However, even this indicator will give you plenty of bad signals if you do not add other filters and trade by simply buying when price hits 200 sma downwards or sell when price hits it upwards.

If you study 4 hour chart of gbp/usd with 200 sma and 200 ema (exponential moving average) below you will see that you would have experienced a lot bad trades. Of course, a lot depends on your stop loss levels, but you do not want to make them a few hundred pips trying to day trade with moving averages. Of course, you would have had some very good trades in the chart, but it would be really difficult to devise a trading system with appropriate risk/reward levels based simply on 200 sma or ema indicators acting as support or resistance levels.

200 sma and 200 ema on 4 hour chart in gbp/usd

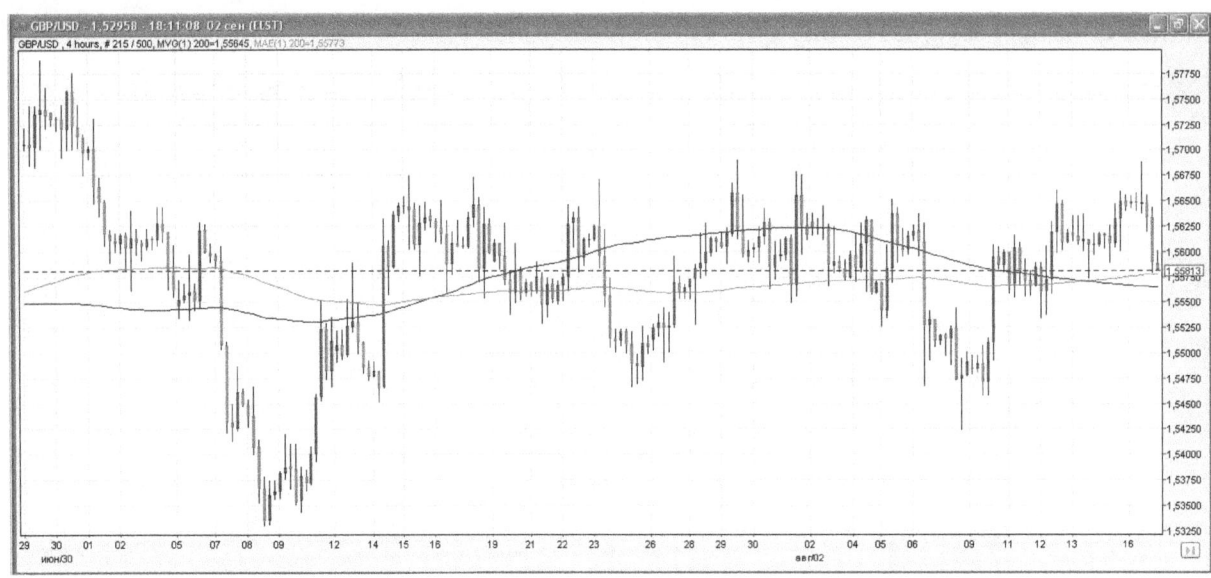

Here is the same time period of gbp/usd, but only on 2 hour chart. You can see that you would have also failed trading 200 sma and 200 ema as support and resistance indicators.

Neither 200 sma nor 200 ema act as support or resistance on 2 hour chart of gbp/usd

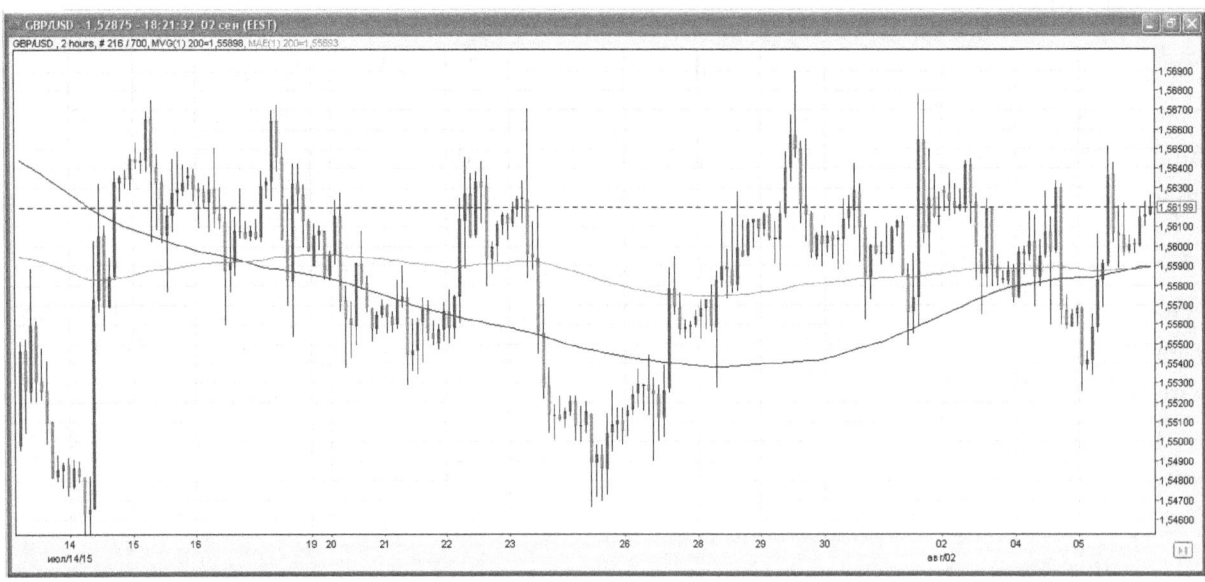

Can we rely on these indicators and if yes, when?

Yes, we can. The main thing that you have to remember is market conditions under which these indicators work. Moving averages are indicators that are to be used when a currency pair is in swing and trend conditions.

Let's look at 1 and 2 hour chart of gbp/usd to see it for ourselves.

2 hour chart of gbp/usd with 200 sma and 200 ema acting as support

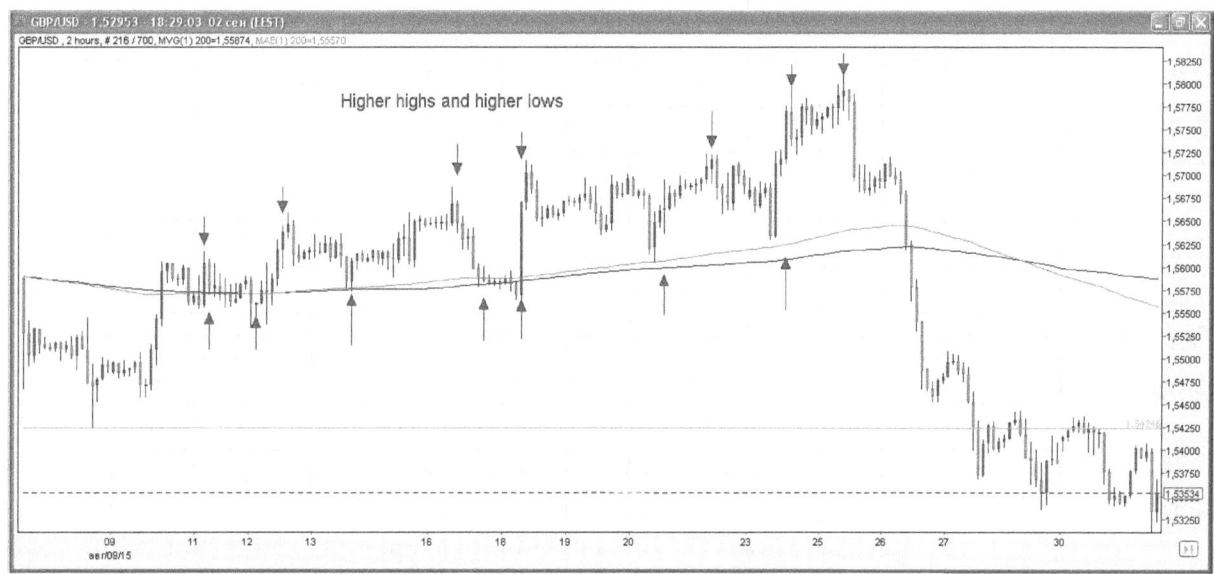

It is obvious that here 200 sma and ema act pretty well as support and resistance levels. However, you can also see that at this particular period of time from the 7th of August, till 25th of August the pair is in an upswing. Higher highs and higher lows are clearly in place indicating that short term trend is up and when there is a trend, moving averages act pretty well.

Below is the same chart of gbp/usd, but of a different time frame (1 hour chart). You might think that you are looking at the same chart and the same time frame as it looks very familiar to the previous one. Yes, it does look familiar, but it is a different time frame. Yet support and resistance is there marked by 200 sma and 200 ema.

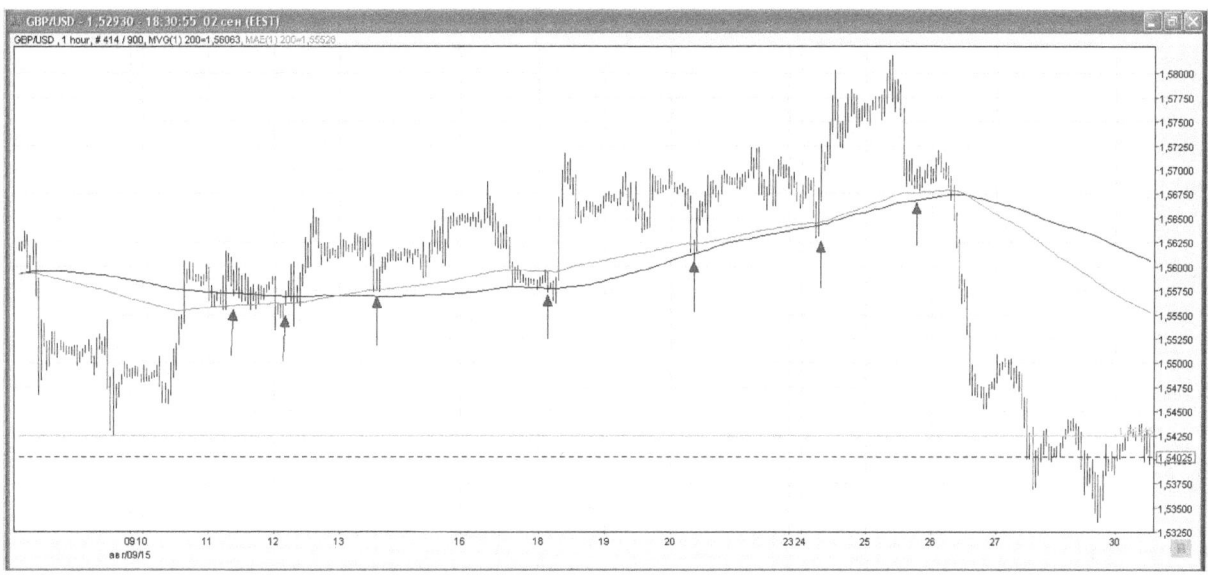

These indicators are almost in the same place as in the previous chart. This is the beauty of the thing.

When you find that 200 sma and 200 ema on 1 hour chart are almost in the same place as in 2 hour chart this will only strengthen the importance of the levels of support and resistance that these two moving averages represent.

So, if market is trending you can trust 200 sma and ema to act as support and resistance more than you could in a range bound market.

For short term moves moving averages of shorter time frames work better than those of longer time frames

In fact, if you see that price is surely moving down day by day you should check where 200 sma and ema are on 15 and 30 minute chart and in most situations you will see that they act as resistance on those time frames often giving you a possibility to enter in the direction of the trend daily.

If you look at 1 hour chart of gbp/usd and take a period from the 25th of August to the 2nd of September, 2015 you will see that the pair is in a short term downtrend (swing down). Now, if you look at the chart just below (15 minute chart) of gbp/usd you will see how well moving averages act as resistance on this short term move. They actually give you two possibilities to enter in the direction of the prevailing trend during the named period on the 31st of August and on the 1st of September, 2015. There were more opportunities, but they were not indicated by moving averages.

200 sma and ema act as resistance in short term gbp/usd move down

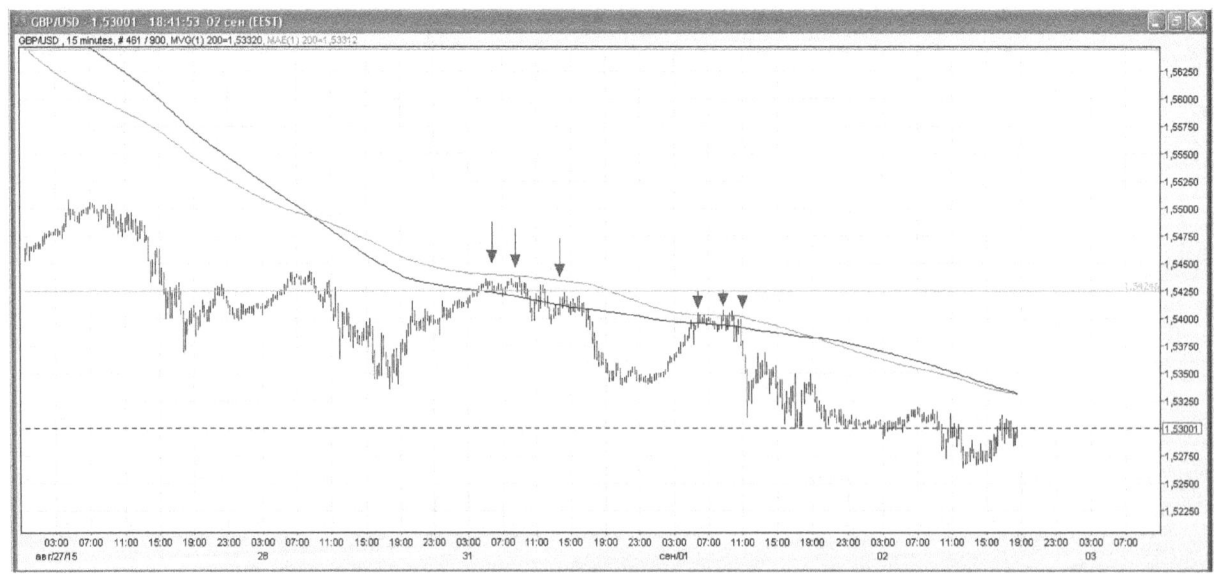

I have also included 15 minute chart of the most popular Forex pair eur/usd. You can spot from the hourly (and also 15 minute chart) that eur/usd was in a short term downtrend from the 25th of August to the 1st of September. And you see how 200 sma acted as resistance in this period on at least 3 (maybe 4) occasions. You could sell the pair when price of it approached the indicator and make a lot of pips.

15 minute chart of eur/usd (200 sma and ema act as resistance on short term downtrend)

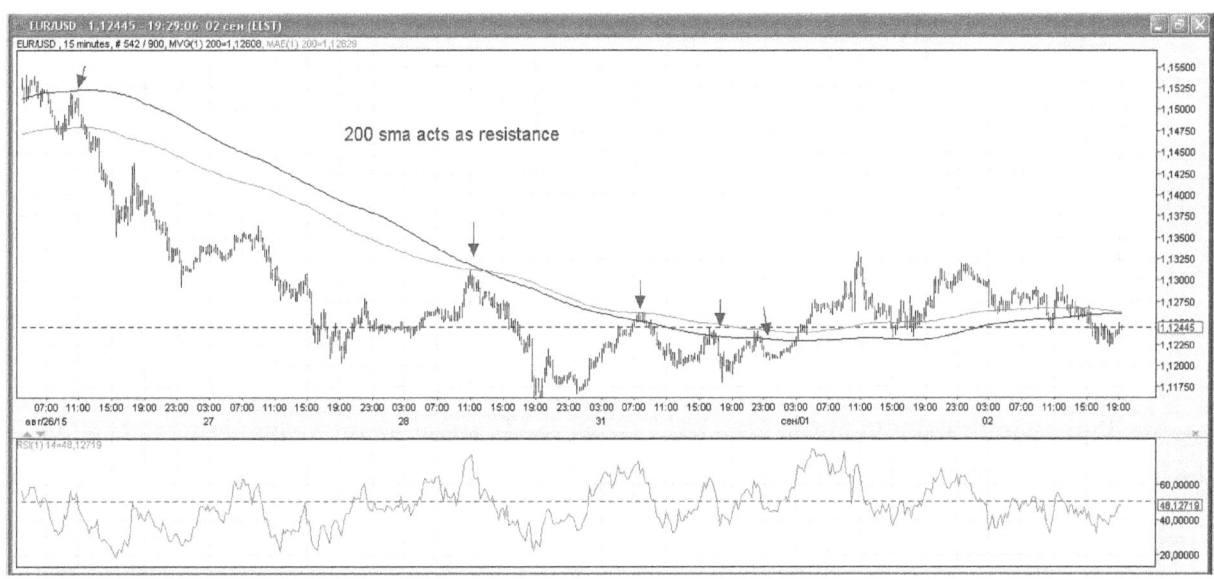

200 sma and 200 ema tend to act pretty well on longer time frames if real tendency is present. Below you can see 4 hour chart of eur/usd. It indicates a period when the pair was in a longer downtrend. Moving averages acted really well as resistance levels and stopped price from rising.

You can see price spike through the averages, but then reverse sharply and downtrend resuming itself. There were four specific situations where a swing trader could enter a short position having seen that the break of moving averages failed and price closed below them.

Look at the chart to see for yourself.

4 hour eur/usd chart (200 sma and ema act as resistance in a longer term downtrend)

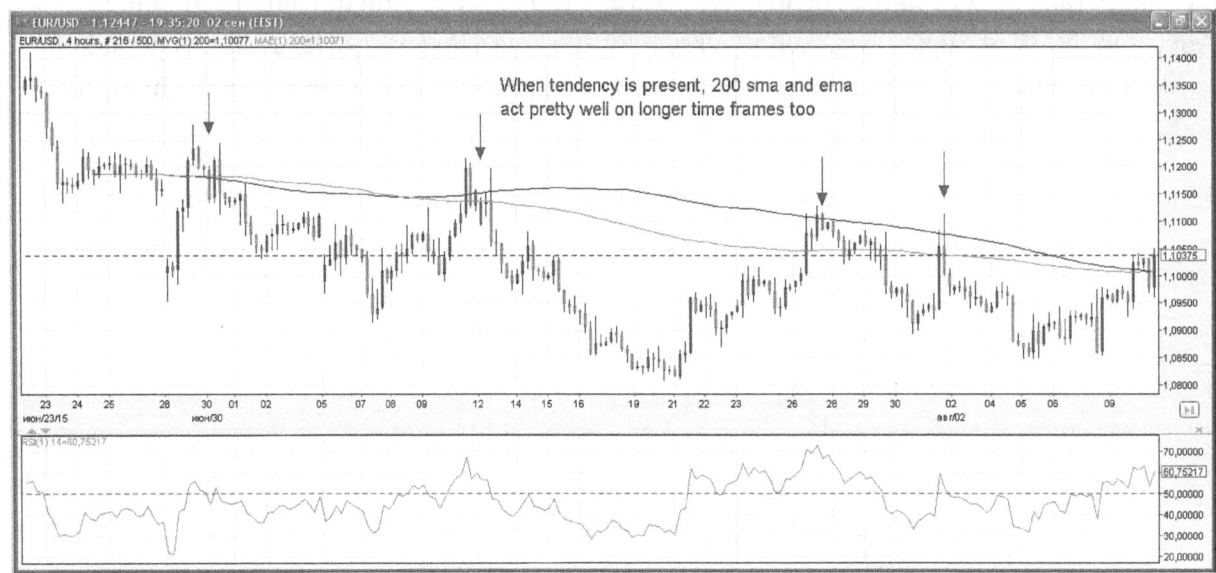

So, we may see that moving averages really work, but mostly in market conditions when there is a prevailing trend. If the trend is up, moving averages will act as support when price falls and if the trend is down, moving averages act as resistance when price rallies upwards.

Using RSI indicator

RSI (Relative Strength Index) indicator is as famous as moving averages. There are a few ways to use it. However, you should also remember that this indicator works under certain market conditions in the same fashion as moving averages.

The most usual way to use RSI is in defining overbought or oversold levels. When the indicator reaches 70 or goes above it, it is considered to be overbought (it is a signal to sell) and when it goes to 30 and below it is considered to be oversold (it is a signal to buy).

However, by looking at the chart below you can see that eur/usd was in a prolonged downtrend and if you bought it when it reached 30 or went below it you would have lost a lot of money.

The downtrend started around June, 2014 and ended only in the middle of March, 2015. Counter trend moves (upwards) were very small and you would have lost more money than you made by buying Euro against US dollar.

RSI went below 30 (on eur/usd daily chart) and stay at that level for a prolonged period of time

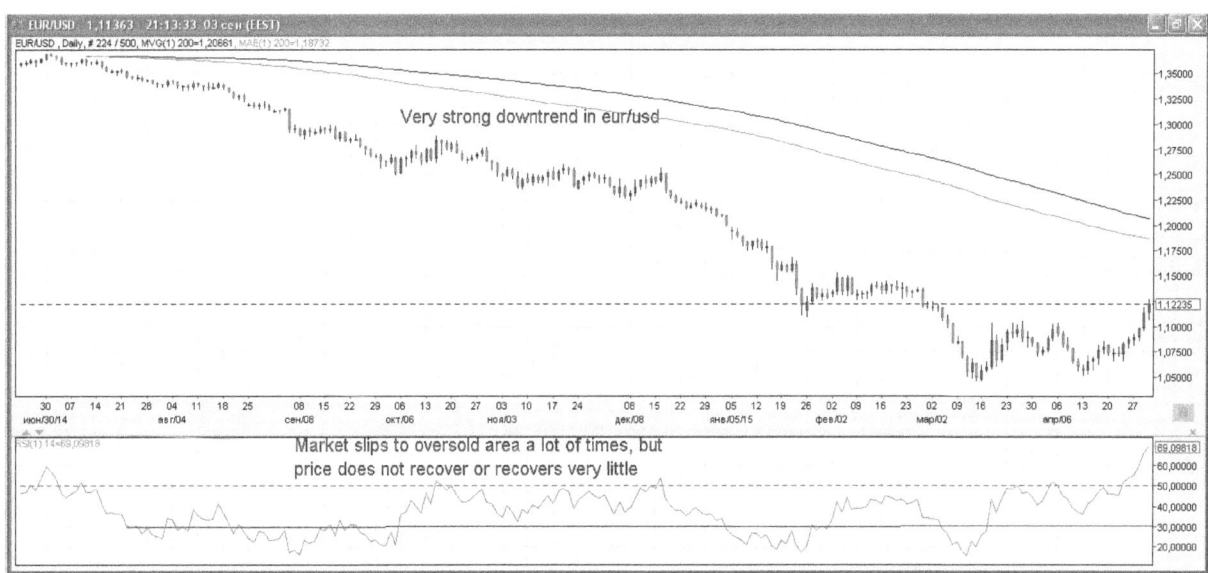

Here is a daily chart of gbp/usd, which was also oversold for a prolonged period of time, but price did not stop from falling for a very long time. Had you tried to buy when RSI touched 30 or went below it you would have lost a lot of money.

RSI stays oversold for a prolonged period of time in gbp/usd

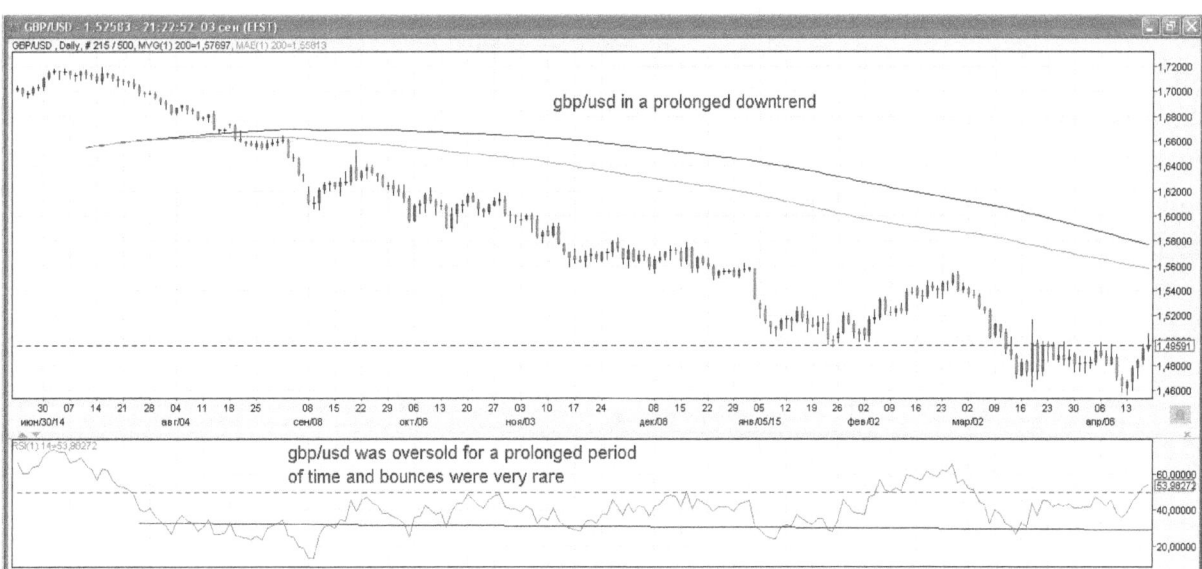

The other most popular usage of RSI is in divergences. A divergence is simply a mismatch between the price and indicator. When price is falling and indicator is rising, it is called a divergence. When price is rising and indicator is falling, it is also a divergence. A divergence simply shows that market momentum is fading and a reversal is about to take place.

However, we can state that this usage of RSI does not work under all market conditions. We may look at the same charts that we used above and see how you would have failed in most cases if you traded RSI divergences under those market conditions.

Below is the same daily chart of eur/usd that was used in the previous page. You can see there were 6 distinct divergences on RSI when price continue making new lows, but no significant turnaround occurred. On the first divergences of the indicator there was actually no rising in price at all.

Daily chart of eur/usd (divergences in RSI fail)

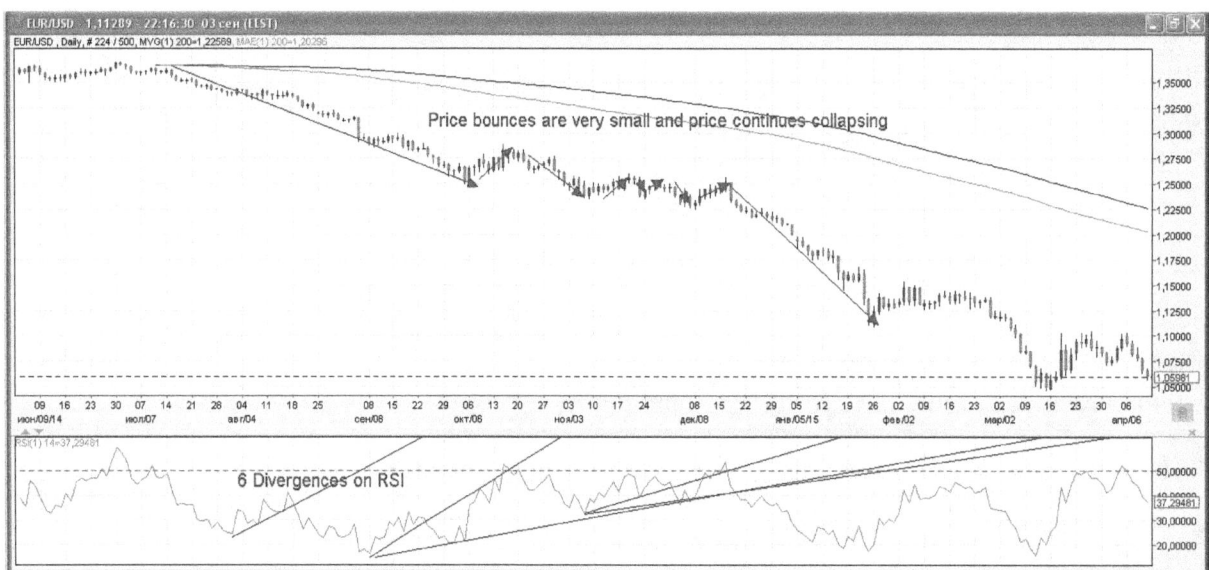

We can also look at the same gbp/usd chart that was used in previous page. Most of divergences did not work out. There was one that sort of worked out. You can see it on the chart. Price rallied around 500 pips after divergence occurred. Others failed to produce any good results. You would have done it wise simply staying aside and not trading against the trend.

6 RSI divergences on gbp/usd Daily chart

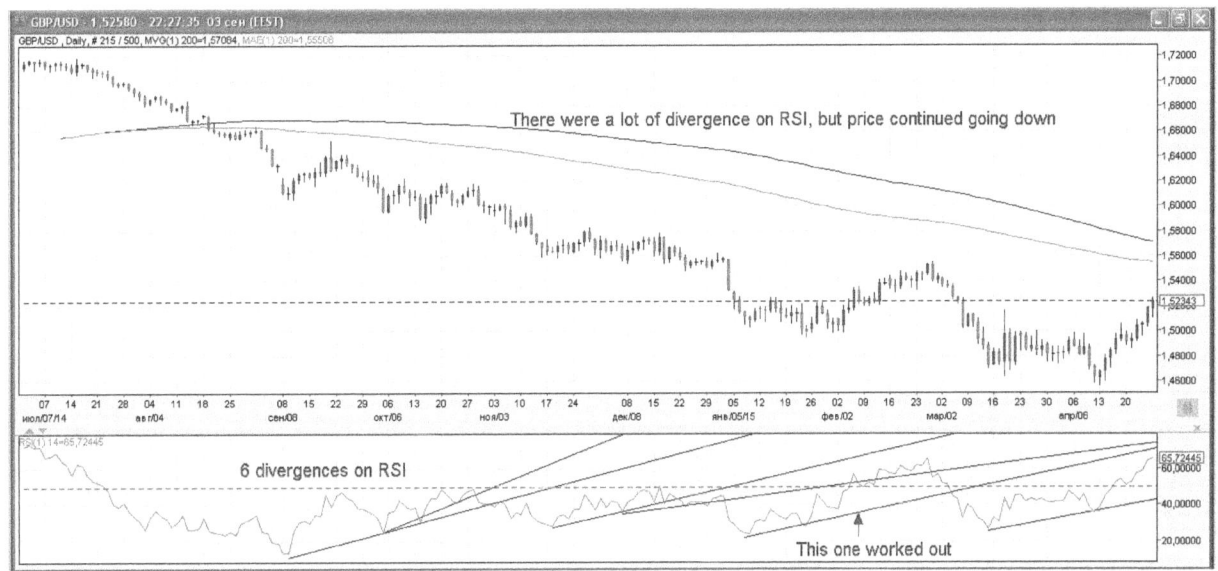

So when do we use RSI correctly?

RSI works best under range bound market conditions. When a currency pair is ranging you can trade both RSI overbought/oversold levels and divergences. You can actually mix those two together to increase accuracy of your trades as well as amount of profit.

Below is the example of aud/usd pair, which was in a range for the most part of July and August of 2015. You can see that in the first case price made a lower low on 4 hour chart in aud/usd, but on indicator you can spot a higher low, meaning that bearish momentum is fading and you should be ready to buy the pair. RSI did not exactly reach 30 (to be oversold), but was very close to that (31). Price rose in a matter of couple of days before making a bearish divergence.

In the second case price made a higher high, but RSI registered a lower high, meaning that bullish momentum is fading and you should be ready to sell the pair. Price started going down the next day.

You would have made money in both cases. In the first case you had to place a buy stop above the first candle that formed after new low was made with a stop loss below the candle. In the second case you had to place a sell stop below the first candle that formed after a new high was made with a stop loss order above the candle.

In the first case you would have risked the same of what you made (100 pips stop loss and 100 pips take profit). In the second case your risk reward ratio would have been much better 1:4 (30 pips of risk and 120 pips of profit, taking into account the high and the low of the range).

Divergences on aud/usd 4 hour chart

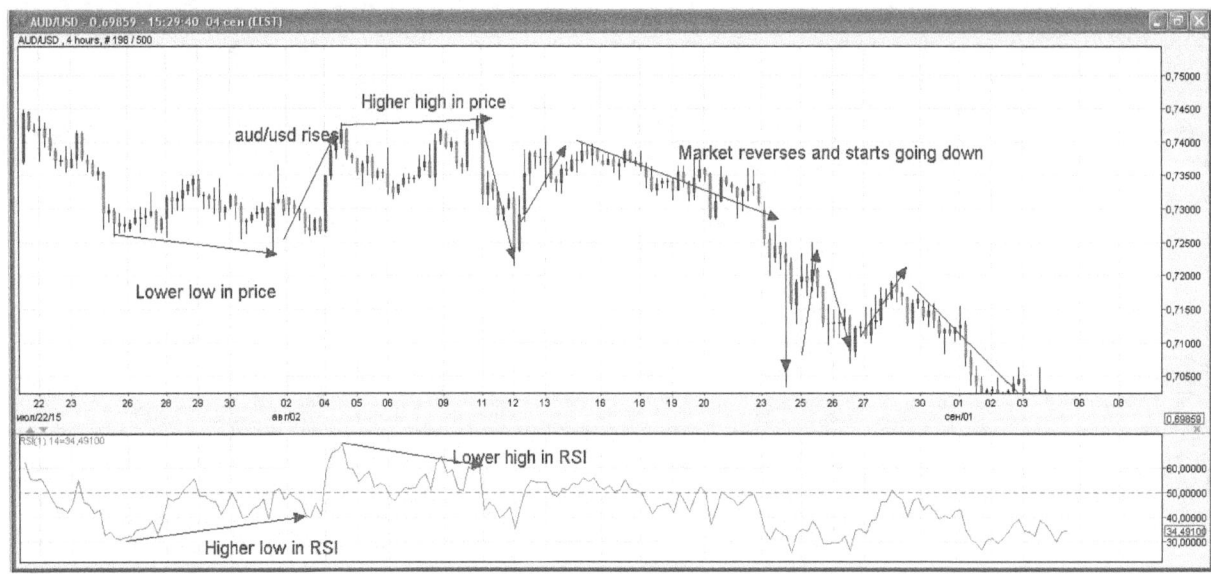

You may look at another chart of usd/cad. If you study usd/cad in more detail you will notice that the pair was actually in an uptrend and trading divergences is not the best choice here. However, if you carefully study the way price rose you can see that it happened in waves and even bearish divergences worked quite well. Of course, bullish ones would have worked much better. You can find more bullish divergences if you scroll the chart.

So, if there is a bias in the market, it is better to trade divergences that show bias towards direction of the prevailing trend and neglecting those that form against it.

Divergences in usd/cad 4 hour chart

Chapter 5

Price action trading, candle patterns and support/resistance

I have already stated in the Ebook, that a lot of professional traders do not use any technical indicators except price action. What is price action trading? It is basically watching what happens around important price levels: support and resistance. Pro traders will watch for continuation or reversals at these levels (depending whether it is a trending or ranging market) and they use various candle patterns to help them.

Traders want to see momentum and a trend happening and then trade in that direction. If it is an uptrend, they would wait for price to dip to important support level, form a bullish candle pattern and this becomes a signal for them to enter the market with a long position.

Conversely, in a downtrend they would wait for price to rally to important resistance level, form a bearish candle pattern and this becomes a signal for them to enter the market with a short position.

How do traders define important support and resistance levels?

Support is a place where price came down and failed to go through it. The level that stops price from falling is support. There might be a false break of the level by some 5-30 pips. It is still a valid support if price rallies and forms a bullish candle.

Resistance is a place where price came up and failed to go through it. The level that stops price from rising is resistance. There might be a false break of the level by some 5-30 pips. It is still a valid resistance if price turns around and forms a bearish candle.

What candle patterns traders watch for?

There are hundreds of candle patterns, but you do not need to know that many. Two or three are enough. The most important thing is that you learn to define them and trade them consistently. The good part is that the same candle patterns can be used in both reversal and continuation patterns.

The most popular candle patterns are: hammers (also known as dojis, pins) and inside candle patterns. These form various combinations and can be named after different names, but the idea behind them all is the same. Let's look at those candle combinations now.

Hammers

A hammer can be either bullish or bearish. Both looks like hammers, except bearish hammer looks like a hammer turned upside down.

Bullish hammer has a long lower wick and a short body at the top of the candlestick.

Bearish hammer has a long upper wick and a short body at the bottom of the candlestick.

Bullish hammer

Bearish hammer

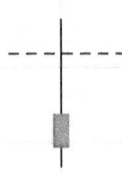

Inside candle may consist of a few (at least one) candles that are within another bigger candle. The biggest candle is often called "Mother candle" and the smaller candle(s) is called "inside candle".

Inside candle pattern

Examples with bullish and bearish hammers

I took a 4 hour gbp/usd chart to show you how well bearish and bullish hammers (and other candle patterns) work in range bound markets at support and resistance levels. In some cases they just come to those levels, form bearish or bullish patterns and reverse. In other cases there are false breakouts and then a bearish or bullish candle pattern and then a reversal.

In the chart below you can spot a lot of bearish candles at resistance. Examine how well they worked and market reversed. You could place a sell stop below each bearish candle (that you see on the left side of the chart) at resistance with a stop loss above the candle and you would have made nice cash on each trade.

You may also see one instance of a false break of support on the 7th of August and immediately a bullish hammer forming. You could simply place a buy stop above the candle and a stop loss below the candle and then go with the flow taking profit at resistance that is marked by resistance line.

In the last example you see a nice bearish candle formation at resistance when a false break occurred and market immediately reversed by forming a bearish candle. It then collapsed without stopping for a few weeks.

Bearish and bullish hammers at support and resistance on 4 hour gbp/usd chart

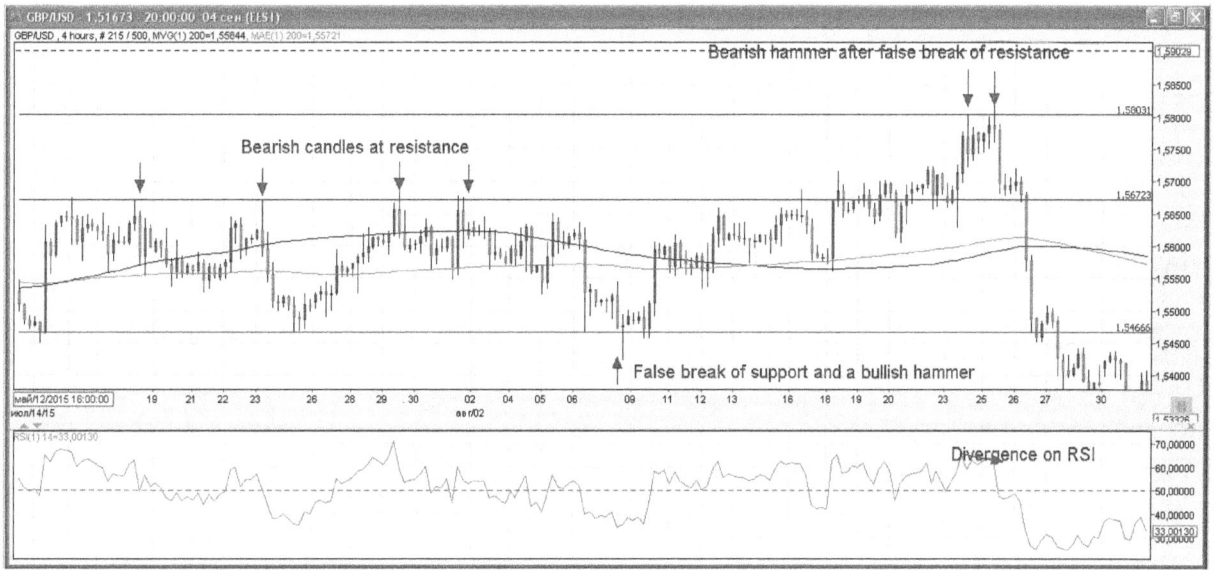

Below is another example with bullish hammers that form in the direction of prevailing trend. The first one lands on important support (previous resistance), the second one at minor support level, but as it is in the direction of the trend.

Bullish pins at support in an uptrend (gbp/usd 4 hour chart)

I wanted to give you one more example with hammers, but this time bearish in the downtrend. The pair is the same: gbp/usd and on the chart you see a short term swing down.

Bearish hammers at resistance in downtrend (gbp/usd 4 hour chart)

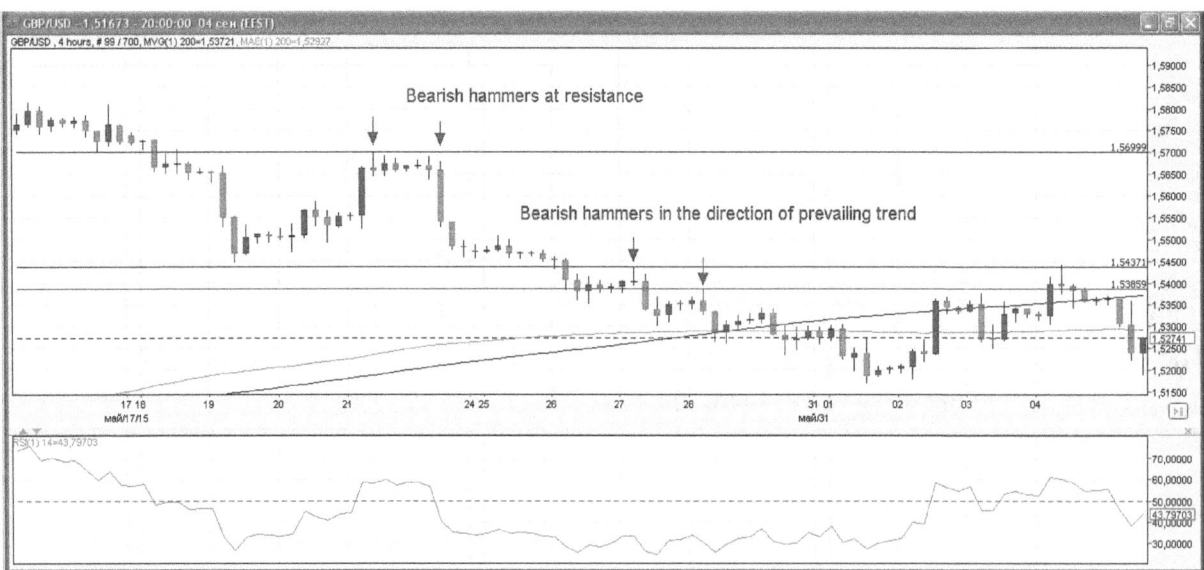

Trading Inside Candle patterns

Inside candle patterns can be used in both range trading and trend trading. As a rule of thumb, you would want inside candle pattern to form near support to go long and near resistance to go short in a range bound environment.

In an uptrend you would also expect price to drop near support, form inside candle pattern and then a break of the mother candle upwards. In a downtrend you would expect price to rally to resistance, form an inside candle pattern and then break of mother candle downwards.

Below is a 4 hour usd/cad chart. You can spot 2 inside candle patterns. Both form near (at) support; therefore you expect a breakout upwards.

You trade inside candle pattern by trading a break of a mother candle.

In the first example we have a mother candle and five inside candles within it. The sixth candle is the breakout candle. You had to trade the pattern by placing a buy stop order above the mother candle and a stop loss below it. Breakout occurred and price rallied over a hundred pips.

In the second example we also have a mother candle with five inside candles within it. There can be just one or two candles. The number is not that important. You had to trade it in the same way as in the first example: place a buy stop order above the mother candle and a stop loss below it. Breakout occurred and price rallied over two hundred pips.

Inside candle pattern in a range (usd/cad 4 hour chart)

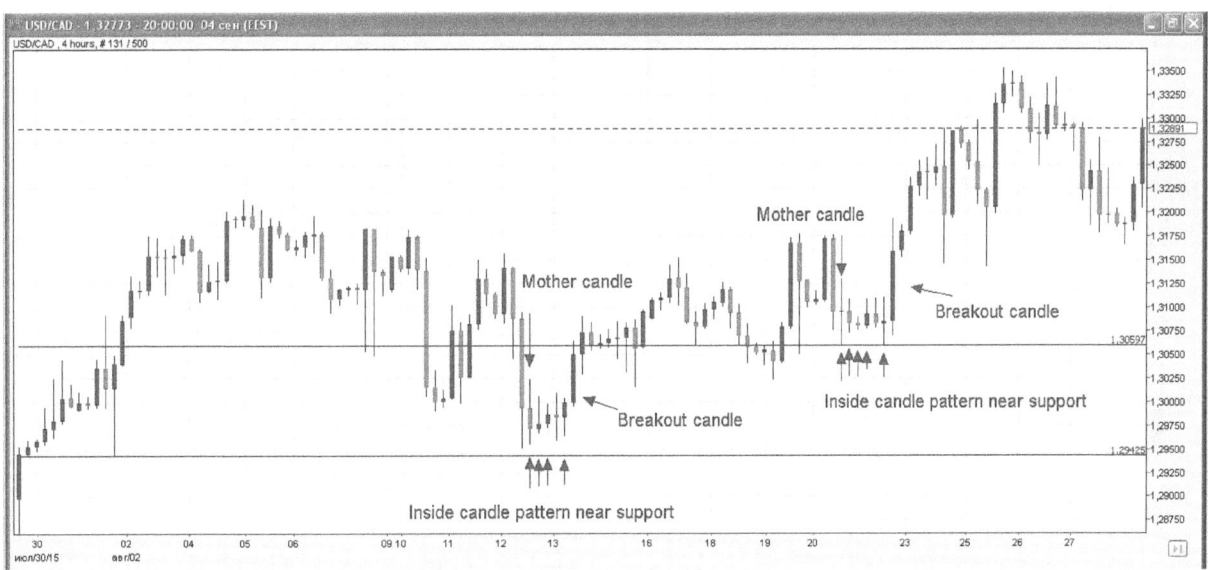

Another example of gbp/usd 4 hour chart shows an inside candle pattern near resistance with a false break of resistance. As you remember, these candle patterns near resistance will most often end with a straight reversal or there will be a false break and price will still reverse to the downside. That's exactly what happened in this example. False breaks of inside candle patterns are often called "fakeouts".

So, an inside candle made a false break up and then reversed immediately. You shouldn't have bought a break up, because at resistance you only wait for price to reverse down, not to go up. But you should have taken a sell below the mother candle with a stop loss above it. Price collapsed around 125 pips from our entry zone to the next support level. That's where you should have closed your short position.

Fake out inside candle pattern on 4 hour chart of gbp/usd

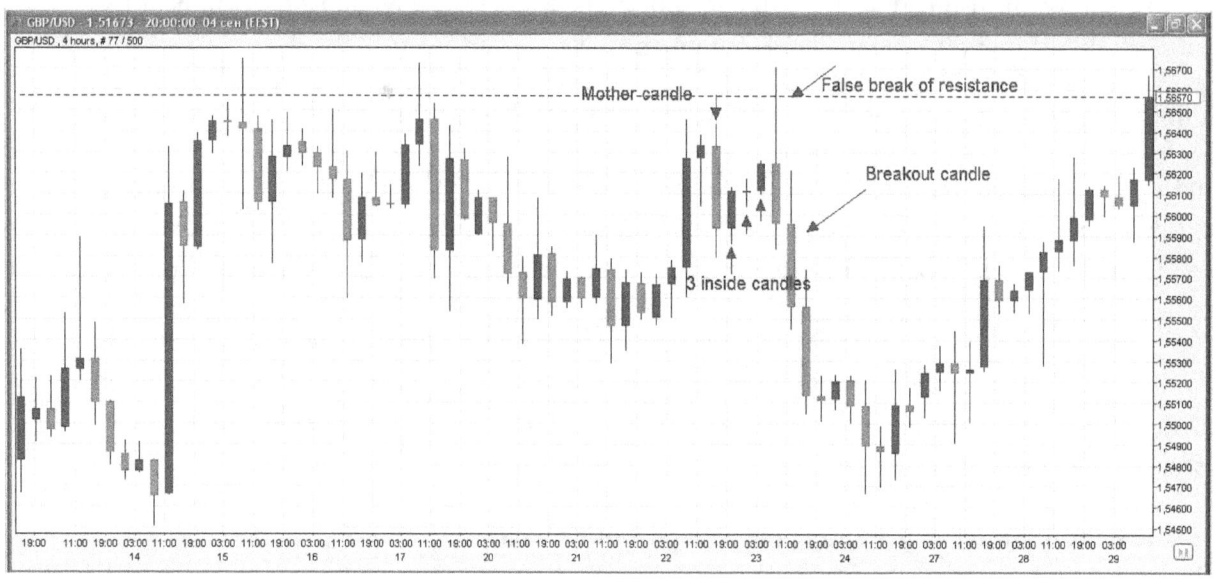

Conclusion

In the Ebook you have learnt that it is important to understand market conditions: trending, raging, choppy. You then have to trade accordingly by choosing the most appropriate trading strategy for that specific market.

I showed you how to identify various market conditions and trade using a specific strategy or stay out without doing anything if situation is not clear.

We also learnt how to identify long term, intermediate and short term market cycles and how to take advantage of that by analyzing each cycle in a specific way and what tools to use to trade it.

Next, we talked about importance choosing the best pair to trade under specific market conditions (the leader) and avoid those who lag behind.

You also found out how to use and how not to use technical indicators in your trades. Again, everything depends on market conditions a given currency pair is in. I singled out moving averages and RSI indicator. You may study how to use other indicators on your own (if you want).

Finally, we figured out how we can trade using support and resistance levels in combination with a number of candle patterns.

I encourage you to continue your studies on your own and also rereading the chapters of the Ebook if you forget certain things. If you want to become a really good trader you should never stop learning.

Good luck!